Ball Cap Nation

A Journey Through the World
of America's National Hat

JAMES LILLIEFORS

CLERISY PRESS

Ball Cap Nation

FOR FURTHER INFORMATION, CONTACT THE PUBLISHER AT:
CLERISY PRESS
1700 MADISON ROAD
CINCINNATI, OH 45206

Library of Congress Cataloging-in-Publication Data

Lilliefors, Jim
Ball cap nation : a journey through the world of America's national hat / by James Lilliefors. -- 1st ed.
    p. cm.
ISBN-13: 978-1-57860-340-4
ISBN-10: 1-57860-340-4
1. Baseball caps--United States. I. Title.

GT2110.L55 2009
391.4'3--dc22

2009009873

Edited by
Jack Heffron

Interior designed by
Stephen Sullivan

Distributed by Publishers Group West

- - - - - - - - -

For Janet

- - - - - - - - -

ACKNOWLEDGEMENTS

Special thanks to Helen Zimmermann, who took on this project, helped to shape the proposal, and found a good home for it.

I am indebted to Jack Heffron, the editorial director at Clerisy Press, who steered this book through the writing, editing, and production phases, and whose editorial suggestions were always on target. I am grateful to the team at Clerisy Press, including Howard Cohen, marketing and publicity director, and Donna Poehner, production manager. And Richard Hunt, Clerisy's president, for deciding to publish it.

The National Baseball Hall of Fame provided valuable assistance with research and photos for the book. Thanks to Senior Curator Tom Shieber, who gave me a tour of the Hall of Fame; Photo Archivist Pat Kelly, for all of her help with photos; and Freddy Berowsky, researcher and head of the reference desk.

Dana Marciniak, corporate communications manager at New Era, was very helpful in arranging interviews, providing photos, and answering questions.

I much appreciate the assistance of Ellen Roney Hughes, Ph.D., curator, and Jane Rogers, associate curator, for the Division of Music, Sports, and Entertainment History, at the Smithsonian's National Museum of American History.

Myra Janco Daniels, CEO and founder of the Philharmonic Center/Naples Museum of Art, inspired me to pursue this project and allowed me the freedom to do so. And I again thank my father and Liliane.

Numerous other people shared their stories and thoughts about ball caps, giving me perspectives on the subject that I hadn't imagined. I am thankful to all of them, and to those who agreed to be interviewed for this book.

I owe a special debt of gratitude to Janet Johnson, who happened to notice one night that so many of our fellow restaurant patrons were wearing ball caps. This book was her idea and I am grateful for her support and contributions along the way.

CONTENTS

INTRO

When I was a kid, baseball caps really *were* baseball caps. There were no designer caps back then. No cap stores in airport terminals. Celebrities *never* wore ball caps. Presidential candidates? Not a chance. There was nothing cool about wearing a ball cap. Look at the newsreel footage from, say, Woodstock, in 1969—or any other big event of the time—and count the baseball caps. There weren't any. The only place you'd see a backwards ball cap in those days was behind home plate, on the head of a catcher.

Our country was different then. If you wanted to wear a ball cap, you had to join a team and play ball. Which was, more or less, the reason I got involved in sports: I wanted to wear the uniform, to be part of the team. I still remember my first sandlot baseball cap—the bright red wool fabric, the authoritative white "M" on the crown, the taut bill that I always curved just a little extra so that it shaded my eyes.

I was, to use a slight exaggeration, an "average" ball player, with a tendency to daydream on the field. I started at shortstop, but they quickly moved me to outfield after a pop fly hit me on the foot. Actually, I was reassigned to what was known as the "far outfield," which was sort of one position beyond the outfielders. The "far outfield" was where they put the players who were left over after the nine starting positions had been filled. Our team had about twenty-seven players in the far outfield, as I recall. Most of what we did out there was kick at the grass, adjust our caps, and think about stuff besides baseball.

DUCTION

Notes From the Far Outfield

On those rare occasions when a ball was hit to the far outfield, we would all look up, in various states of panic, waiting to see who would step forward to catch it. Some of the far outfielders would do a little dance-and-squint routine, pretending to be getting in position to make the catch. But no one ever did. Once the ball thunked to the ground, we would all run toward it and the one who got there first would pick it up, look at it briefly, and then throw it in the general direction of where we imagined the infield was. Then the real outfielder would take over, although by that point the batter had already rounded the bases at least once. Occasionally, when all of the far outfielders were daydreaming simultaneously, a ball would actually hit one of us.

The league I belonged to was called the MBBL, which stood for Manor Boys Baseball League. I have no idea who the "Manor Boys" were, or why the league was named for them. As I recall, anyone whose parents were willing to pay the "equipment fee" was accepted in the league. At that age (I was nine and a half, going on ten, as we used to say), kids were expected to join stuff, to find out where they fit and where they didn't. Some were fortunate to discover their callings right away—in this case, they became the pitchers and the home-run hitters; the rest of us wound up in the far outfield. But the good part of the deal was, we all got to wear the caps (and being a member of the team also gave us a license to wear our caps off the field, a license I used liberally).

Our team was known as the Senators, which happened to also be the name of our Major League Baseball team at the time—the Washington Senators (an inspired name, reportedly chosen over such formidable runners-up as the Congressmen, the Vice Presidents, and the House Ways and Means Committee). The teams we played were named for MLB clubs, too, most of them referring to birds, Native Americans, or sock colors.

The sandlot Senators actually beat the big-league Senators once, incidentally, in a historic night game at D.C. Stadium, by a score of, I think, thirty-seven to nothing. Well, okay, not *technically*. We never really *played* the Washington Senators. But people used to say that we *could* beat them if we ever did. That's because the Washington Senators of the mid- to late-1960s were about the worst team in the history of baseball. Their combined batting average was something like .0057 and their earned run average was, I believe, 21.7. They were the Hamilton Burgers of big-league baseball. There was a saying about the Senators back then: "Washington—first in War, first in Peace, and last in the American League."

As a kid, though, I didn't get that. Not at all. I always thought the big-league Senators were on the verge of a spectacular turnaround—like those fallen comic book heroes who suddenly found a hidden reservoir of strength which enabled them to rise up and pummel the bad guys into submission.

Even when the season was winding down, and the Senators were a hundred and fifty games behind, I would listen faithfully each night, sitting under the stars on our back porch in the D.C. suburbs, a nine-volt transistor radio pressed to my ear, my heart thumping as the game went into the top of the ninth with the Senators down by something like 21–0 and Frank Howard coming to the plate.

One of the saving graces about the big-league Senators, my father liked to point out, was that some of the teams that came to Washington to beat the crap out of us really *were* good. Several times each

The author, right, at age five, wearing his first cap, shares a
wagon with his younger brother.

summer he'd take us downtown to see the Senators play the Yankees,
for instance, and we'd get to watch such legendary players as Mickey
Mantle, Roger Maris, and Whitey Ford. That didn't excite me a whole
lot, though. I was too loyal to the Senators. (In 1972, the Washington
Senators were sent away to Texas for rehabilitation, a process that involved, among other things, being co-owned for several years by
George W. Bush. It took thirty years before another baseball team came
to Washington. There's a saying about this new team, which is called
the Nationals: "Washington—first in War, first in Peace, and last in
the National League.")

Of course, the sports world was a smaller place then. We had great
athletes, but we didn't yet call them "superstars." Television networks
didn't pay billions of dollars a year to broadcast baseball and football

games. Endorsement deals didn't double or triple the annual Defense Department budget, as they do now. Merchandising was a modest side business; fans didn't walk around wearing caps and jerseys advertising their favorite teams.

In fact, if you *did* wear a cap, of any sort, back then, people tended to think you were a little strange. My mom—who was a wonderful person in every other way—sometimes wore a sad, droopy little cotton ball cap to keep the sun off her face, and it embarrassed at least one of her children to no end. Then there was the old guy at the hardware store who wore a ratty looking yellow mesh-style cap—which was invariably off-kilter and unfastened in the back, as if someone had mistaken his head for a hat rack and just set it there. He always sat in a lawn chair by the front window of the store, by the seed displays, staring out at the parking lot. The first few times we saw him, my friends and I would walk back and forth out front trying to decide if he was "real" or not.

There was also a man named Mr. Hadler (or "Hadler," as my father called him) who lived down the street from us. Mr. Hadler had to be one of the creepiest people in the D.C. area back then (not counting elected officials). He rarely came out of his house, but always stood behind the screen door, it seemed, smoking a cigarette and watching the street. Whenever we rode past on our bicycles, there he was. We knew very little about Mr. Hadler except that there was a faded "Goldwater" sticker on his car and that the police had gone to his house one night, after he "roughed up" Mrs. Hadler. I overheard my father saying this to my mother, and, of course, had no idea what "roughed up" meant. But it further enhanced the notion in my mind that Mr. Hadler was of a different—possibly alien—species. (Mrs. Hadler, in case you're wondering, was never seen; the only thing we knew about her was her name: Mrs. Hadler.)

On the rare occasions when Mr. Hadler did come outside, he wore a dirty white T-shirt, carried a can of Pabst Blue Ribbon, and had the strangest-looking thing on his head. It was a ball cap, but unlike any I had seen or would see again—grungy, sweat-stained, of indeterminable color. The reason he came outside was to look at the bushes beside his house and say "Shit" several times.

The only other occasions when I would see ball caps in those days were on our road trips through the Midwest. My father liked to stop at those open-all-night restaurants along the turnpikes, where we would all sit at the counter and have a slice of pie and ice cream and a soda at some ungodly hour of the night. I never felt safe when we did that; I always imagined that the other customers were conspiring to rob us, tie us up, and steal our car. Typically, there would be three or four truck rigs parked outside and two or three men sitting at the counter. The men would be unshaven and drinking coffee, mumbling to themselves, and occasionally staring at my mom. Many of them wore a low-rent cousin of the baseball cap, also known as the "trucker cap."

And that was it. Besides my mom, only oddballs, aliens, and truck drivers wore ball caps (I should mention here that some of my favorite people are truck drivers). But it was a situation that would change dramatically during the 1970s, for reasons that some of our best minds are still trying to explain. After several ridiculous headwear fads came and went—the "floppy" hat, the headband, the oversized knit cap—baseball caps gradually became acceptable and then, inexplicably, fashionable.

By the mid-1980s, ball caps were becoming a fad, and a burgeoning industry. In 1992, even our Presidential candidates wore them, presumably to show their kinship with the common man and woman. Bill Clinton and Al Gore jogged together wearing their ball caps. George Herbert Walker Bush—at the time known as "George Bush"—wore one on the campaign trail that read, "The Other White Meat." (Yes, he *did*.)

In true American style, people soon began wearing them inappropriately, as well—backwards, sideways, indoors, and even in church (see Chapter Eight, "Cap Etiquette"). Caps had become, in a sense, cultural equalizers. When President George W. Bush snuck away from his Texas ranch in 2003 to visit the troops in Iraq for Thanksgiving, his escape was enhanced by the use of a ball cap. These were the President's own words: "I slipped on a baseball cap, pulled 'er down—as did Condi. We looked like a normal couple." The classical violinist Joshua Bell in 2007 donned a ball cap, jeans, and a T-shirt and stood by the escalator at the L'Enfant Plaza subway stop in Washington, D.C. for forty-five minutes, playing some of the most gorgeous music ever written. Bell routinely sells out Carnegie Hall, but nobody in Washington even stopped to listen for more than a few seconds.

Yes, caps have become an easy way of seeming "normal"—the goal of a growing number of Americans, apparently. Throw on a ball cap before you go to the store and no one will give you a second look, regardless of what's underneath. If you haven't shaved or your skin is full of blemishes, the clerk won't pay you any mind. If you have two mouths or a tentacle where your left eye should be, no worries. We're all just normal folks when wearing our ball caps.

Many theories have been proposed as to why we've become a "Ball Cap Nation." The salient one, of course, is that ball caps finally solve a problem that has stymied great thinkers for decades—bad hair days. But does the ascendancy of the ball cap also reflect some fundamental change in the structure of our thoughts and feelings over the past three decades? What does it really mean that we have become a Ball Cap Nation? What does it say about our values, our priorities, and our character? Once you start asking these sorts of questions, it is inevitable that other, related questions will arise. "Why has the ball cap culture spread so rapidly around the world?" for instance. "What's with the sideways ball cap?" And, of course, "What are the advantages of drying a wet baseball cap on your head?"

All of the above questions will be addressed in these pages. Our experienced reporting team traveled around the country in search of answers, speaking with cap historians, manufacturers, retailers, sociologists, collectors, and an out-of-work vending machine repairman. We visited a few famous cap-wearers, several almost-famous cap-wearers, and a couple of clearly-never-will-be-famous cap-wearers. We even asked former President George W. Bush what he thinks our cap-fixation says about American society, particularly during the eight years of his administration. You can just imagine his answers (you'll have to, because he declined to respond to our queries).

As our country has grown increasingly diverse and complicated, we have sought—and, occasionally, found—things that unite us. The ball cap feeds an idea that we, Americans, seem to cherish: As different as we all are—despite the fact that some of us stand on the pitcher's mound while others loiter in the "far outfield," kicking at the dirt—when we wear a ball cap, we're all part of the same team.

1
BORN IN THE USA

The invention of a national pastime;
how the ball cap was born
and raised on America's baseball fields;
a visit to the "birthplace"
of baseball; and an interview
with a baseball uniform historian.

OVER the past thirty years, the baseball cap has emerged as America's national hat, evolving from a sports accessory to a universally accepted part of our casual wardrobe. No one knows exactly why this happened.

The ball cap is by far the most popular headwear apparel in the United States today, accounting for more than 80 percent of hat sales, according to some estimates. Moreover, it has been adopted by virtually every social stratum in the country, from disaffected teens to celebrities to software moguls to middle-aged, middle-class moms and dads to retirees. Nearly everybody in the United States owns at least one ball cap.

If the cap has become a part of our collective national uniform, though, there is nothing uniform about why or how it is worn. We wear ball caps to make a statement; to show an allegiance; to shade our eyes from the sun; to look and feel sporty or hip; to be a part of something larger than ourselves. We wear them backwards, forwards, and sideways, tilted at various angles. They are a simple but ingenious product—inexpensive, utilitarian, and aesthetically appealing.

An American invention, the baseball cap is now worn and sold in most countries around the world. Along with blue jeans and Coca-Cola, it has become one of our most ubiquitous cultural symbols. Internationally, ball caps are a two- or three-billion dollar industry, which has roughly doubled in size every few years since the early 1980s.

How ball caps ascended to such prominence is a question with no simple, single answer. Nor can we say with certainty where the cap-wearing trend will lead or how long it will last. But we do know where the ball cap came from: It was born on the fields of America's "national pastime."

Like baseball itself, early ball caps were derived from existing models—among them cricket, jockey, and military caps. But in the mid- to late-nineteenth century, as the country began to distinguish itself on the world stage, baseball took on a uniquely American personality, complete with its own unifying rules, its own traditions, its own venues, and its own uniform. The baseball cap as we know it today—with the six-panel crown, visor, and top button—has its roots in this era.

The idea that baseball is America's "national sport" first began to circulate in the decade before the Civil War (on the heels of such ideas as American exceptionalism and Manifest Destiny). Baseball was one of a number of factors that stitched together our disparate, still-fledgling country, helping to assimilate droves of immigrants and to strengthen the identities of America's cities. In some ways, the story of how the cap evolved parallels the story of how the country evolved.

To learn the origins of the baseball cap, we went first in search of the origins of baseball—journeying into a rich and rolling land of lore, where the scenery is often awe-inspiring but seldom to be trusted. We begin with a visit to baseball's "birthplace"—Cooperstown, New York, and the National Baseball Hall of Fame.

BIRTH OF BASEBALL

Baseball was invented, the story goes (or, went), in the tiny village of Cooperstown, New York, in 1839. The inventor of the game was a twenty-year-old Army cadet named Abner Doubleday. On a summer afternoon in 1839, Doubleday pulled a stick through the dirt in Elihu Phinney's cow pasture—once, twice, thrice, four times—tracing the outlines of a baseball diamond, then extended the first- and third-field lines to create an outfield. He scratched marks in the dirt to show where the fielders stood, and later wrote out a set of rules describing how the game was played. Doubleday also came up with the name for this new sport: "base ball."

Those were the findings, anyway, of a group called the Mills Commission, which was convened in 1905 to determine baseball's origins. The commission's findings, summarized in a report released on the next-to-last day of 1907, stated that, "according to the best evidence obtainable to date, (baseball) was devised by Abner Doubleday at Cooperstown, N.Y. in 1839."

The report concluded, "In the years to come, in the view of the hundreds of thousands of people who are devoted to baseball, and the millions who will be, Abner Doubleday's fame will rest evenly, if not quite as much, upon the fact that he was (baseball's) inventor ... as upon his brilliant and distinguished career as an officer in the Federal Army."

At the time, baseball was not only America's national sport; it was also becoming a thriving national industry. Six years earlier, the American League had been launched, challenging the hegemony of the National League, which had monopolized professional baseball since 1876. The National League was created by a group of team owners and managers who realized that they could make more money by

MAJOR ABNER DOUBLEDAY,
Of Fort Sumter.
Entered according to Act of Congress in the year 1861, by M.B. Brady. in the
Clerk's office of the District Court of the U.S. for the So. District of New-York.

Abner Doubleday, the "inventor" of baseball,
according to the 1907 Mills Commission report.

pooling resources and controlling who was allowed in the league—a
business model that set the pattern for professional sports leagues in
America, which continues today. The introduction of eight American
League teams in 1901 (in Baltimore, Boston, Chicago, Cleveland, Detroit, Milwaukee, Philadelphia, and Washington) led to two years of
bitter rivalry between the leagues. But in 1903, sensing that both sides
would benefit by joining forces, the American and National Leagues

staged the first "World Series," and a new, larger monopoly was created. (In that first, best-of-eight series, American League pennant winners the Boston Americans (later the Red Sox) upset the National League's Pittsburgh Pirates 5–3.)

As the sport grew more widespread, its uniform became increasingly standardized. Gone was the smorgasbord of cap styles that followed the earliest straw hat days. At the time of the Mills report, the pillbox cap, popular in the 1880s and 1890s, had been replaced by what would become the modern-day baseball cap.

Baseball had developed from the gentlemanly, upper middle-class club game of the 1840s and 1850s—a game modeled on English cricket—into a highly competitive, commercially driven spectator sport. Early wooden baseball stadiums—known as baseball parks, grounds, or fields—came along in the 1860s, with bleacher seating for hundreds and eventually thousands. Hilltop Park, where the Highlanders (later the Yankees) played from 1903 to 1912 in upper Manhattan, had a capacity of sixteen thousand with room for ten thousand standing patrons. The first steel-and-concrete stadium, Shibe Park in Philadelphia, opened in 1909, with seating for twenty-three thousand.

Baseball gradually took on the grain of the country. *The Book of American Pastimes*, the first comprehensive study of sports in America, noted, "(Baseball) is a game peculiarly suited to the American temperament and disposition ... it has an excitement and vim about it." That was 1866. Two decades later, the American poet Walt Whitman said, "Baseball is our game, the American game ... I connect it with our national character."

Baseball was a game made for heroes—a team sport that emphasized the individual. Its symbolism was suitably American: each man taking his turn, standing alone, with an equal but limited number of chances to hit back whatever life threw at him. Baseball was a microcosm of the American dream, and the stage for a burgeoning American mythology, played out in the long shadows of late afternoons on grass-and-dirt fields in front of bleachers filled with thousands of people who dressed up for the occasion.

The actual origins of the sport, though, had been disputed for many years. Newspaperman Henry Chadwick, a cricket reporter who began covering baseball in 1856, was one of the game's early boosters—he may have been the first to use the term "national pastime"—but he didn't buy the idea that baseball was an American invention. Chadwick, born in England, maintained that the sport was simply a variation of longstanding English ball-and-bat games such as rounders.

For many Americans, who took pride in their nascent national sport, the notion that baseball may have originated in England seemed decidedly unpatriotic. It bothered no one as much as former baseball-star-turned-sporting-goods-impresario Albert Spalding. Big and blustery, with a brush mustache and a flair for self-promotion, Spalding had been a pitcher for the Boston Red Stockings and the Chicago White Stockings, who compiled a career won-loss record of 253–65. Shortly before retiring as a player in 1878, he and his brother started a sporting goods business that would become the country's largest. As a player, team manager, and owner, Spalding was one of the most influential men in the sport for about thirty years.

Spalding was friendly with Chadwick, but the men disagreed on the origins of the national sport. After Chadwick made the case, in a 1903 article, that baseball was really an English game, Spalding responded by creating the Mills Commission. The commission consisted of Abraham Mills, former president of baseball's National League and Spalding's longtime friend; Morgan Bulkeley, a U.S. Senator and the National League's first president; James Sullivan, president of the Amateur Athletic Union; Alfred Reach and George Wright, sporting goods distributors and former ball players; Arthur Gorman, a former player and president of the Washington Base Ball Club; and Nicholas Young, also a former National League president.

The commission advertised across the country, seeking input from anyone who had knowledge or information about the invention of baseball. For two years, letters came in, mostly from former ball players. But the commission did little legwork or follow-through. Its report, which included a dissenting comment from Chadwick, was nevertheless widely accepted for several decades.

The notion that baseball was born in Cooperstown was bolstered in 1934, when a small, homemade baseball was found in a farmhouse three miles from the village. This ball, people in Cooperstown began to speculate, might, indeed, have been the game's first. The misshapen ball, which became known as the "Doubleday Baseball," was purchased by a wealthy local resident named Stephen Clark, who displayed it in town.

If baseball had been invented in Cooperstown in 1839, as the Mills Commission determined, then its centennial was fast approaching. Clark and several baseball officials, including National League President Ford C. Frick, and American League President William Harridge, began planning an event that would mark the anniversary. Frick proposed a Hall of Fame shrine in Cooperstown. In 1936, the first Hall of Fame election was held and five inductees were chosen: Babe Ruth, Ty Cobb, Honus Wagner, Christy Matthewson, and Walter Johnson. By then, the mythology of American baseball had been enhanced by such stars as Ruth, Lou Gehrig, and Jimmie Foxx. The low-scoring, so-called "dead ball era" of 1900 to 1919 had given way to the home-run era of the 1920s, when, for various reasons, baseball became a much more exciting, and lucrative, spectator sport. The proliferation of radio in the 1930s further boosted baseball's fortunes. Everyone, it seemed, followed the game. Baseball players were national heroes, and the National Baseball Hall of Fame and Museum, which opened in Cooperstown on June 12, 1939, seemed a fitting monument to America's game.

AMERICA'S GAME

The only real problem with the Mills Commission report was that its findings were completely bogus. The "best evidence" cited in the report was actually based on a single source: the testimony of a seventy-one-year-old Colorado miner named Abner Graves, who claimed to have witnessed Doubleday invent the game back in 1839, when Graves was a five-year-old living in Cooperstown.

Doubleday, though, was not actually *in* Cooperstown during 1839; he was a cadet at West Point for the whole year. He went on to become a national war hero, seeing action in the Mexican-American War, the Seminole Wars, and the Civil War where, as a Union general, he played a key role in the Battle of Gettysburg. When Doubleday died in 1893, there was no mention in his *New York Times* obituary of baseball. Nor did he write about baseball in any of the sixty-seven diaries that he left behind.

Although the Mills report described Graves as "a reputable character," other accounts cast him as a fanciful storyteller. Toward the end of his life, Graves shot and killed his second wife, and he spent his final days in a mental institution.

The objective of the Mills Commission—most of whose members were friends of Spalding's—wasn't to settle the controversy over baseball's origins so much as it was to quiet it down. Their report accomplished that, even though its findings are no longer taken seriously. The National Baseball Hall of Fame, which wouldn't be where it is without the report, even has an exhibit discrediting the Mills Commission. But in many ways it had the elements of a perfect yarn—that baseball had been invented in a small, idyllic lakeside village in rural America, in a town founded by Judge William Cooper, the father of *Leatherstocking Tales* author James Fenimore Cooper; and that its creator had been an American war hero, who was no longer around to comment on it one way or the other. Although the story had no more basis in fact than Parson Weems' account of George Washington chopping down his father's cherry tree, it fed into the mythology of baseball—and literally created a shrine to the sport. It had been Spalding's goal to show that baseball had "an American dad." The Mills Commission did that, at least for a while.

The Mills Commission report came along during a pivotal decade for America's national sport—when the American League doubled the size of baseball to sixteen teams (a number that would hold until 1961) and the World Series was begun. It was also the decade when the ball cap became standardized. The baseball cap was one of the features that gave the sport its distinctive look. Baseball was, and still is, the only American sport with an official uniform that includes a cap.

Gradually, baseball historians chipped away at the Cooperstown myth. In 1953, the United States Congress credited Alexander Cartwright with "inventing" baseball in the 1840s. Cartwright, a bookseller and fireman, had started the Knickerbocker Base Ball Club in New York in 1842 and four years later drew up a set of rules that many believe established modern-day baseball. On June 19, 1846, the first officially organized American baseball match was played at Hoboken's Elysian Fields between the New York Base Ball Club and the Knickerbockers (the New York Base Ball Club won 23–1, with Cartwright umpiring).

But, in truth, baseball's origins substantially pre-date 1846—or 1839, for that matter. Several years ago, the first known documented use of the term "base-ball" in the United States was discovered at Pittsfield, Massachusetts—in the form of a 1791 ordinance, banning the play of "base ball" within eighty yards of the town square, "for the Preservation of the Windows in the new Meeting House." When the ordinance was discovered, Pittsfield Mayor James Ruberto proclaimed, "Pittsfield is baseball's Garden of Eden." Mentions of "base-ball" also appear in American newspapers from the 1820s.

The earliest known reference to baseball came from England, though, in a 1744 children's book called *A Little Pretty Pocket-Book*. A German book on sports games, published in 1796, included a section on

"English base-ball." And Jane Austen's first novel, written in 1798 and 1799, contained this sentence: "No more cricket, no more base-ball, they are sending me to Geneva." Most baseball historians now agree that baseball was adapted from English bat-and-ball games.

Perhaps the real origins of baseball go back even earlier, though. On a wall at the National Baseball Hall of Fame is a 1251 AD drawing of Spaniards playing a game with a ball and bat, which bears a superficial resemblance to baseball. Next to it is another, much older image, a wall relief from the shrine of Hathor, in a temple at Deir-el-Bahari, Egypt. It shows Thutmose III, a pharaoh who ruled Egypt in the fifteenth century BC, holding a ball in one hand and a long, wavy-looking stick in the other. The hieroglyphic over the image says, "Batting the ball for Hathor."

Peter Piccione, an Egyptologist and professor of comparative ancient history at the College of Charleston in South Carolina, gives a talk titled "Pharaoh at the Bat" about this early game. Piccione believes that the Egyptians were the first people to play "bat-and-ball" games.

Of course, there are no known stats on Thutmose III, who became Egypt's ruler as a boy and reigned for almost fifty-four years. Nor is there any footage of Thutmose and his cronies playing ball. But one can sort of imagine it: The youthful Thutmose stepping up to the plate, wearing his customary kilt and headdress (first precursor to the baseball cap). He is a slightly rotund young man with spindly legs, whom the workers call "Babe" because of his boyish looks. He points his wavy-looking bat in the direction of the Pyramid of Giza and calls his shot.

Swings at the first pitch.

The workers turn.

It's going …

They begin to run.

Going …

Back, back, back …

It's …

Alexander Cartwright (top center), with members of the New York Knickerbockers. In 1849, the Knickerbockers wore the first recorded baseball uniform, which included straw hats.

THE NATIONAL SPORT'S CAP

Even if baseball's origins were not truly American, we adopted baseball and made it our own. Similarly, the baseball cap, which went through various trials before becoming standardized, borrowed elements of existing caps.

The first official baseball uniform was that worn by the New York Knickerbockers on April 24, 1849. Records show that it consisted of blue woolen pantaloons, white flannel shirts, and chip straw hats. In the 1860s, as semiprofessional baseball began to take root, particularly in New York City, an early version of what we know as the baseball cap, with a bill and a curved crown, was born.

Here are ten evolutionary signposts on the road to the modern-day professional baseball cap:

Boston/Brooklyn Style

The Brooklyn style hat, worn by the Brooklyn Excelsiors in the 1860s, was, in some ways, the forerunner of the modern ball cap. This cap incorporated elements of other hats, including the jockey cap and military hats. A similar cap, advertised in Spalding Guide, was called the Boston Style Cap. Both featured a small brim and a round, forward-leaning crown, with a button on top joining the stitching. The earliest cap in the National Baseball Hall of Fame, from 1866, is similar to these caps. This style was not widely worn until the late 1890s.

Pillbox

A more popular design was the "Chicago style" pillbox cap, with a flat top, a short bill, and horizontal or vertical stripes. This style, derived from military caps, was the most popular when the National League was formed in 1876 and continued to be widespread throughout the 1880s and the 1890s.

Letters and Logos

Letters identifying team names and home cities began appearing in the 1880s, although they did not become widely used until the late 1890s. The first big-league club to put an image of the team's nickname on its cap was the Detroit Tigers in 1901. That cap featured a running orange tiger.

The last big-league team to don a cap without a letter or a logo was the 1945 St. Louis Browns, who wore a white cap with thin orange and brown stripes.

Air Holes

Air holes in the crowns of baseball caps were not a feature in the pillbox hats, but appeared in other ball caps during the 1890s. Their function was to allow air to enter the cap and cool the head on hot days. Air holes became a regular part of the baseball cap by the first decade of the twentieth century.

An advertisement for "Base Ball Caps" from the 1888 edition of Spalding's Official Base Ball Guide.

Standardization

The standardized look of the "baseball cap" was not realized until about 1900. Early sports catalogues show a variety of hats under the broad heading "base ball caps." An ad from an 1888 Spalding catalogue, for instance, includes ten different styles, including hats that could be described as a beanie, a conductor's cap, a derby, a jockey's hat, and what appears to be a layer cake with a visor. Standardizing the uniform became a way of standardizing the game. By the turn of the century, the pillbox-style cap was on its way out, and an ancestor of the current-day ball cap was in widespread use.

Stitched Visor

In 1903, Spalding introduced the Philadelphia-style cap, which was the first to feature a stitched visor. The stitching attached the fabric of the bill to the cardboard insert. This soon became a regular part of the ball cap.

Six Panels

In many early ball caps, the crown was made of eight separate panels. The six-panel cap became more common in the late 1880s, although it wasn't standard until well into the twentieth century.

Longer bills

The bill gradually became longer in the 1920s and 1930s, providing a more pronounced shading effect (all baseball games were played during the day until 1935). The visor also became firmer, changing from cardboard to latex rubber, which was in general use by the 1940s.

Vertical Crowns

In the late 1940s, the crown of the baseball cap became more vertical. A weave of cotton fibers called buckram became the stiffening agent used to reinforce the front crown panels and is still a part of MLB caps. The vertical crown made the team logo more prominent and also gave the cap a more aesthetically pleasing look.

Polyester

Caps were made out of wool for most of the history of Major League Baseball. But other materials changed. The leather sweatband, for instance, became cotton in the 1920s. The most recent change to the Major League baseball cap came in 2007, when the standard cap changed from wool to a polyester fabric. The change was made to better manage sweat, reduce shrinking, and reduce odor. The new cap was designed to "wick" sweat—spread it across the fabric, then absorb and evaporate it. The new caps retail for thirty-two dollars, three dollars more than the old ones.

EXPORTING BASEBALL

America's version of baseball, invented in the 1800s, soon spread to other countries, carrying with it some elements of the American spirit and, yes, the American baseball uniform. Baseball was introduced to Cuba, for instance, in the 1860s by Cuban students studying in the United States. It became popular in other Caribbean-region and Latin American countries, including the Dominican Republic, Puerto Rico, and Venezuela. It is played professionally in all of these countries today.

Baseball and its cap were introduced to Japan in the early 1870s by an American teacher, Horace Wilson. The country's professional baseball league was launched in 1920. Over the past fifty years, baseball has been Japan's most popular spectator sport.

BEFORE PEOPLE THOUGHT THAT WAY

*"We shouldn't say baseball invented this cap, but I think it would be fair
to say that baseball solidified its place in our culture."*
– Tom Shieber, Senior Curator, National Baseball Hall of Fame

Beneath the National Baseball Hall of Fame in Cooperstown is a treas-
ure trove of memorabilia—storage vaults and rows of shelves containing tens of thousands of artifacts, including caps, uniforms, bats,
gloves, and balls. There are several aisles filled with boxes of old Major
League game-worn baseball caps, some of them dating to the nineteenth century. Tom Shieber, the Hall of Fame's senior curator, leads
a private tour of this remarkable subterranean baseball museum.

Shieber, an expert on the history of baseball uniforms, has created
an online exhibition called "Dressed to the Nines," which traces the
year-by-year development of the baseball uniform. Most of it is based
on hours spent poring through old ads from Spalding catalogues and
other sports publications.

Normally, when an item comes to the Hall of Fame, there is little
accompanying information; it is the job of Shieber and the curatorial
staff to determine what role, if any, the artifact played in the history
of baseball.

"Our job really is to tell stories," he says. "There's a story to everything
here. But it often takes a lot of research to put those stories together."

Wearing white gloves, he displays one of the gems of this storage
area: the Hall of Fame's oldest New York Yankees cap, dating from
1912. Technically, it isn't really a Yankees cap, it's a Highlanders cap.
The team wasn't officially named the Yankees until 1913, even though
fans called them that for several years. The logo on this cap is similar
to that on the current Yankees cap; but this cap has a looser crown
and a shorter brim.

It was donated to the Hall of Fame in 1990, Shieber says, by a

Baseball Hall of Fame Senior Curator Tom Shieber with boxes of game-worn
MLB caps, in the storage vault below the Hall of Fame.

little-known former Highlander player named Paul Otis. Several
months after donating the cap, Otis passed away. His signature, "P.
Otis," can be seen on the cap's sweat band; but Shieber determined
that Otis had probably signed the cap right before giving it to the Hall
of Fame. As he inspected the cap further, he noticed that another name
was also written in the band: "Dolan."

"This cap does match the 1912 cap. I looked up Paul Otis' record
and the times he played. What I found was that he was with the team
very briefly. Literally for only five games. Then I found out that Cozy
Dolan also played with them in 1912. What happened was Dolan
played with them early in the season, and they brought Otis out of the
minors later on and gave him the cap."

Neither player is recognized today, but there is an interesting history
to this cap, Shieber says. "The Yankees played in a benefit game right

after the Titanic sank (on April 14, 1912). Dolan was there for that game, sitting on the bench. And I also found out that Dolan was in the lineup for the first game at Fenway Park, on April 20, 1912. So he almost certainly wore this cap during the first game ever played at Fenway Park."

Shieber, who worked as an astrophysicist for UCLA's astronomy department for a dozen years before joining the Hall of Fame ten years ago, shared some of his thoughts about the evolution of the baseball cap:

BCN: Where did what we now call the baseball cap come from?

TS: What we can say is that the baseball cap developed over a period of time and that it came from different sources. The first hats were straw, but baseball was a different game then. Baseball started out as a club sport, as a social get-together, a fraternal group. The earliest baseball uniform was more a club uniform than a sports uniform. As the game changed, the cap took on more functional purposes—it shielded the eyes, and it also identified the teams—but there were many different styles. We do know that when the National League started, in 1876, and into the 1880s, the pillbox style was the most popular.

BCN: That's the cap that the Pirates brought back for the 1976 centennial of baseball?

TS: Yes. Actually, what happened was in 1976 a number of National League teams, not all, wore an imitation of the pillbox-style cap to celebrate the anniversary. The teams all went back to their regular caps the next year. The Pirates didn't get the message. They continued to wear it for several years and actually won a World Series wearing it in 1979.

BCN: Why did the pillbox-style ball cap fade away?

TS: There are functional reasons and there are fashion reasons. Exactly why some of these styles went out of fashion is unclear. Sometimes there are obvious influences that cause a change in what teams wear. When the University of Michigan basketball team started wearing the baggy uniforms, it caught on, it went up to the pros and that's the standard today. With the baseball uniform, it has tended to be more subtle and more gradual. Often if a certain player or a winning team does something that's a little different, it catches on.

BCN: Do you have any favorite baseball caps?

TS: I liked the halo on the top of the Los Angeles Angels cap in the early sixties. That was innovative. The Angels had an idea, went with the theme, and it became part of their identity. The other one was the "scrambled eggs" design on the Seattle Pilots cap. Those were two inspired caps. I'm an old-school kind of guy, but I don't mind experimentation with uniforms.

BCN: What were the most significant changes to the baseball cap during the twentieth century?

TS: The longer bill and the vertical crown were the two significant developments. The vertical crown made sense—you could see the letter or the team logo better. It also set the stage for commercial caps, such as John Deere and Caterpillar. It helped make the cap a forehead billboard.

BCN: Ball caps are worn everywhere now off the ball field. Why has the cap grown so popular over the past thirty years?

TS: I don't know if it's possible to know why. I would say in part it's a style-driven thing, but it's hard to trace.

BCN: Now that most MLB games are played at night, what is the functional purpose of the baseball cap? Is there any reason for the visor, for instance?

TS: That's something I'm looking at right now. Would a player be as good or better if he didn't wear a baseball cap? Is it even beneficial? I don't know. In other sports—in swimming or track, or bicycling, for instance—efforts are made to shave every second off your time by streamlining your equipment and uniform. Baseball's origins go back to long before people thought that way. Caps are a tradition. Are they necessary? That's a good question.

THE MODERN CAP

The look of the baseball cap hasn't changed substantially since the mid-1950s, when the New Era company introduced its 59Fifty—the cap used by all Major League Baseball teams. Most ball caps worn casually today are similar in appearance to those of professional baseball, although they tend to be a cotton blend rather than polyester, to be less structured, and to have adjustable one-size-fits-all bands.

What *has* changed is people's attitudes about the ball cap and about its role in our culture. Baseball caps may have been born on America's ball fields, but they're worn now for reasons that have nothing to do with baseball. This change in attitude was the result of a quiet American revolution that has not yet made its way into our history books. We'll call it the Cap Revolution.

2

THE CAP REVOLUTION

How the baseball cap morphed from a sports accessory
to a symbol of American culture; eight forces that
converged to create the Ball Cap Revolution.

"It has long been my conviction that we can learn far more about the conditions, and values, of a society by contemplating how it chooses to play, to use its free time, to take its leisure, than by examining how it goes about its work."
– *Bart Giamatti, former President of Yale University and seventh commissioner of Major League Baseball*

UNTIL the late 1970s, wearing a ball cap anywhere but on the baseball field carried with it a cultural stigma—a stigma reinforced by decades of American films and television shows, which often depicted cap-wearers as comical or marginal characters. In the mid-1930s, Scotty Beckett pioneered the sideways/backwards ball cap look in the *Our Gang* comedies (a look likely inspired by Jackie Coogan's oversized wool cap in Charlie Chaplin's 1921 film *The Kid*). Huntz Hall portrayed the buffoonish Horace Debussy "Sach" Jones in the Bowery Boys movies from 1946 to 1958, with his trademark flipped-brim ball cap. The style was adapted in the 1960s by backwoods mechanic/gas station attendant Gomer Pyle on *The Andy Griffith Show* and was parodied in the 1970s by Rick Nielsen of the rock band Cheap Trick. Then there was the Beav—Theodore "Beaver" Cleaver—who frequently wore an unlettered ball cap on the 1957–1963 sitcom *Leave It to Beaver*. And Oscar Madison, the slovenly half of *The Odd Couple*, who donned a Mets cap in the 1968 movie (when the Mets were still loveable losers) and on the 1970s television show. Not to mention Klinger on *M*A*S*H* in the 1970s, with his Toledo Mud Hens cap. In 1976's *Carrie*, mean girl Norma Watson wore a red baseball cap throughout the film (even to the prom), whacking Carrie with it in the film's opening sequence.

There are other examples—but few, if any, before 1980 portraying cap-wearers as heroes or sex symbols. For the longest time, baseball caps simply got no respect. Baseball players wore caps, of course, but there was a clear demarcation between the world of the professional athlete and the world of the civilian spectator.

The liberation of the ball cap, then, was also the uprooting of an entrenched cultural stereotype. As with many revolutions, the Ball Cap Revolution seemed to happen quickly—although, in fact, it was years in the making. What follows are Eight Factors behind the Cap Revolution—eight separate cultural currents (whose sources flow back as far as post-World War II) that reached a confluence in the 1980s, making it acceptable, and then fashionable (and, in some cases, maybe even heroic) to wear a baseball cap.

FACTOR 1
The Marriage of Sports and Television

The union of sports and television in the late 1940s and early 1950s began a partnership that would nudge professional sports toward the center of American society and ultimately create the American Sports

Culture, a multi-billion-dollar industry that would demand not only our attention but also our participation. And, it would lay the ground-work for the sports merchandising boom of the 1980s.

Television made sporting events more accessible to more people. As TV technology improved, it also made them more nuanced, so that the experience of watching a game on television was nothing like watching one in person. In the late 1940s, baseball was broadcast from three static cameras, all located on the mezzanine level; there were no zoom lenses; one announcer gave the play-by-play. Sports broadcasting steadily became more sophisticated and, eventually, cinematic: We saw the game from mul-tiple perspectives, up close and high above; we saw plays repeated, in super slow motion; we saw the facial expressions of the players on the field—grinning, grimacing, concentrating, cursing. Television made the game and the players seem life-size, and it put them in our living rooms. It continues to do so—with high-definition and giant-screen televisions. In 2008, a football game between the San Diego Chargers and Oakland Raiders was even screened in 3-D—trumpeted as an initial step toward regular 3-D sports broadcasts. Why not? Writer Michael Arlen famously called Vietnam the "living room war" because it was the first war that unfolded on our tel-evision screens (TV was still in its infancy during the Korean War). With the rise of television, American sports became the Living Room Game.

It happened quickly: When the first World Series was televised in 1947, an estimated 3.9 million people watched (many of them in bars), as the Yankees beat the Brooklyn Dodgers four games to three. It was by far the largest television audience up to that point. Less than 1 per-cent of American households had a television set in 1947. But by 1955, 67 percent of U.S. households had TV sets; and by 1960, almost 90 percent did. Television united the country as the Internet would in the 1990s, although it provided much more limited choices. With only a handful of stations, we all watched the same shows, and sports became a major part of the equation. By the mid-fifties, all sixteen teams in Major League Baseball had television contracts.

Big-league sports expanded dramatically in the television age, creating new markets and giving more people "home teams" to root for and support. In 1960, Major League Baseball fielded sixteen teams, the same number as in 1901. It added eight more in the 1960s (Los Angeles Angels and Washington Senators, 1961; New York Mets and Houston Colt .45s, 1962; Seattle Pilots, San Diego Padres, Montreal Expos, and Kansas City Royals, 1969). Today, Major League Baseball has thirty teams.

The cost of television contracts for all major sports soared in the sixties and seventies. So did salaries. In 1975, Major League Baseball players were granted the right to free agency, meaning they could negotiate with any club in the league after a one-year option on their contracts expired. Salaries jumped. In 1975, the average MLB player earned just $44,600 (about $94,500 in 2008 dollars). Ten years later, the average salary was up to $369,000 ($714,000). Last year, the average salary was more than $2.4 million.

As the cinematography of sports broadcasting continued to evolve, and salaries approached those of movie stars, we began to see sports differently—as entertainment and as big business, not just as athletic competition. The most-watched television program each year became the Super Bowl, and the main draw for many of those who tuned in were the commercials, not the game. The business of sports depended on fans and outside sources to keep it growing. The notion that professional sports would enhance a community's economic development and social status led to additional franchises in new markets and taxpayer-subsidized stadiums. Sports became a central part of cities' identities. We embraced and supported our home teams, and in doing so showed loyalty to our communities. A sports mythology took hold in America, which affected how we thought, how we interacted with one another, and what we wore. In this environment, people were ready to buy products advertising their favorite teams. It was just a question of making them available.

FACTOR 2
Grassroots Baseball

At the same time that television was transforming big league sports, Little League, and its sandlot cousins, were proliferating in small towns across America. In 1947, the year the first major league World Series was televised, Little League held a World Series of its own—its first. Little League ball had sixty teams that year and about a thousand players. Ten years later, almost half a million boys were playing in the Little League on 19,500 teams in forty-seven states. There are now about 200,000 Little League teams in all fifty states and eighty countries.

Founded by a Pennsylvania lumberyard clerk in 1939, Little League brought baseball—and the baseball cap—to small-town boys throughout the nation (girls, alas, weren't allowed to play until 1974). Many boys wore their caps off the field, as well, during a period when hat-wearing in general was in decline.

Millions of teenagers, meanwhile, wore baseball caps on the fields of American Legion Baseball, which was begun in 1925 in Milbank, South Dakota, and became a national program the next year.

Minor League Baseball also flourished after the Second World War, with attendance jumping from ten million in 1945 to thirty-two million the next year and forty million in 1949. At its peak, minor league ball was played in more than three hundred cities in the country. Interest declined in the fifties, for various reasons, including television; it surged again in the 1970s, and in recent years has approached its peak year of 1949.

Grassroots baseball widened the game's scope, making it a participatory sport—and, in the process, validating cap-wearing at levels other than just the big leagues.

FACTOR 3
Promo Caps: One Size Fits All

While Grassroots Baseball took the game—and the cap—into small-town America, an unrelated trend scattered the ball cap throughout rural America.

In the late sixties, a new promotional accessory known as the "company cap" emerged—a cheap, plastic mesh ball cap with a tall, foam front emblazoned with a company logo. The caps featured a snap-lock, plastic tab on the back, so that one size fit all heads.

Conceived as an advertising ploy, company caps were typically given away to customers and potential customers. Agriculture businesses were among the first to use the promo caps, along with auto dealers and manufacturers. But businesses were surprised to find people requesting the caps, and some companies began selling them. A spokesman for John Deere said that orders for the company's signature green-and-yellow caps increased about 40 percent a year in 1974, 1975, and 1976 before leveling off.

In 1978, the *Chicago Sun-Times* took note of this trend: "The company cap is one of the hottest advertising and promotional tools for the nation's companies, from giant Caterpillar to local bait shops," the paper noted. "Brightly colored and bearing a patch with a company's logo, the cap has outclassed—if not outnumbered—T-shirts and occasionally turned into a collector's prize. For companies like DeKalb AgResearch, Caterpillar, International Harvester, Goodyear, and Ford, the cap has been a promoter's dream. Take a trip into the countryside and see them sprouting from nearly every head."

K-Products, one of the largest company cap producers of the time, reported selling about 300,000 caps a week in 1978.

Promotional caps had nothing to do with the American Sports Culture, but they made the ball cap accessible in America's heartland and an accepted advertising tool in the business world.

FACTOR 4

Sunscreen

Coco Chanel supposedly popularized the suntan when she fell asleep on the deck of a yacht off the southern coast of France in 1923 and returned to shore looking startlingly bronzed. When branded suntan lotion came on the American market in the 1940s, its purpose wasn't sun protection, it was tan enhancement. One of Coppertone's early ad campaigns depicted an Indian chief and the slogan "Don't Be a Paleface." In 1953, Little Miss Coppertone first appeared on billboards in Miami. The soon-to-be-iconic illustration showed a cute black dog tugging down the swim trunks of an adorable, pig-tailed blonde girl, revealing her pale derriere. Later sunscreen ads featured sultry, deeply tanned models. To be tan in those days was to be young and beautiful.

In the 1970s, suntanning was still one of America's favorite idle-time activities. But concerns about skin cancer were mounting, causing

By the 1980s, the ball cap was becoming a popular form of protection from the harmful rays of the sun.

some people to rethink their sun-worshipping ways. In 1972, the Food and Drug Administration reclassified suntan lotion from a cosmetic to an over-the-counter drug. Two years later, a Swiss chemist adapted a system he called Sun Protection Factor, or SPF, which measured how effectively suntan lotion protected skin from the sun's ultraviolet rays. In 1978, with skin cancer rates climbing, the FDA created the SPF measurement system and issued this warning: "Overexposure to the sun may lead to premature aging of the skin and skin cancer." By the 1980s, the term suntan lotion had been replaced by sunscreen.

Like cigarettes—which American culture promoted for decades as being cool, sophisticated, and sexy—suntans could lead to some very uncool consequences. As people became more and more aware of this, they grew skittish about the sun. For protection, they slathered on high-SPF sunscreen and, often, wore hats. Because the baseball cap was cheap and its brim shaded part of the face, many people developed the habit of wearing a ball cap when they went outdoors as a means of sun protection, and to keep the glare from their eyes.

FACTOR 5
The Magnum Effect
From 1980 to 1988, Tom Selleck starred as Thomas Magnum on *Magnum, P.I.*, the CBS television series about a Hawaii-based private investigator. Magnum was the first television hero and sex symbol to regularly wear a baseball cap. Beginning with an episode titled "China Doll" (broadcast December 18, 1980), Magnum frequently wore a Detroit Tigers cap, with the famous Old English "D" logo on the crown. Selleck was a Tigers fan in real life.

His wearing the cap on *Magnum, P.I.* did two things: It made sporting a ball cap seem cool rather than quirky; and it created an interest in authentic MLB caps, which by the end of the eighties would be doing a bang-up business.

Thomas Magnum was a Vietnam veteran who also wore a VM02 cap on the series (for those keeping score, it was first seen in the episode "Tropical Madness" from November 12, 1981). The VM02 cap came from Magnum's stint with naval intelligence in Da Nang during the Vietnam War. It should be noted that he also occasionally wore a red-and-white "Al's Collision and Muffler Shop" cap. No fooling.

Once Selleck had broken the cap ceiling, so to speak, other TV characters were seen in pro-sports caps, including former Oakland cop Mark Gordon (Victor French) on *Highway to Heaven* (1984–1989), who often wore an Oakland A's cap; and McGyver (Richard Dean Anderson), the secret agent and adventurer from the show of the same name (1985–1992), who wore a black-and-red or white-and-red Calgary Flames hockey cap.

Now, of course, many celebrities are often seen wearing pro (particularly Yankees) ball caps. A website called Capitate has a gallery of famous people—from Madonna to Bill Clinton to Chris Rock—wearing the caps of their favorite teams.

But it started with Thomas Magnum.

FACTOR 6
Buying In: The Merchandise Boom

In 1978, the New Era cap company placed an ad in *Sporting News* newspaper for authentic Major League Baseball caps. At the time, New Era and Sports Specialties were the two major licensed manufacturers of pro-ball caps. (Sports Specialties, also the first licensee of the National Football League, was founded in 1928 by David Warsaw who, among other things, invented the bobble-head doll. The company, a pioneer in the field of licensed sportswear, was sold to Nike in 1993.)

This was New Era's first attempt at mail order and as company historian Karl Koch recalls, "We had to shut it down, there were too many orders coming in. These weren't people who went to games.

They were out in the middle of Iowa and places like that. It was an early sign that people wanted this."

At the time, merchandising was still a relatively modest side business. Accessories and souvenirs were sold at games, but the sale of official products was otherwise very limited. In the 1980s, this would change.

Large-scale merchandising was the logical next step in the American Sports Culture. It built the culture in two ways: first, it created a new revenue stream; second, the products creating that revenue stream advertised the culture. Getting people to buy a product that serves as an advertisement for itself is a pretty sweet deal if you can pull it off.

In 1986, MLB and New Era teamed up to produce the Diamond Collection, which officially sanctioned the on-field product. "'Wear the caps the pros wear' became the idea," Koch says.

Professional sports was a shared national passion by then, which played out in millions of living rooms across the country. Wearing apparel sanctioned by the big leagues brought fans closer to the action and closer to one another; it was an investment in their teams. The ball cap market seemed a natural—and it was.

FACTOR 7
Patriot Caps

In the mid-1980s, another trend attracted a very different sort of cap-wearer. After a decade clouded by war, political scandal, gas shortages, and runaway inflation, a new mood of optimism and patriotism settled over much of the country in the early 1980s. In a speech given on March 8, 1983, in Orlando, Florida, President Ronald Reagan first used the phrase "evil empire" in discussing the Soviet Union and what he called "the struggle between right and wrong and good and evil." The next year, Tom Clancy's Cold War thriller *The Hunt for Red October*—a book Reagan strongly endorsed—became a No. 1 bestseller. The image of the American military, tarnished by the Vietnam War

Rob Reiner, as director Marty DiBergi, wore this variation of the USS Coral Sea CV-43 cap in the 1984 film *This is Spinal Tap*.

years, gained new luster during the Reagan presidency. People felt good about their country.

The public supported substantial increases in defense spending during this time and became increasingly interested in books and films pertaining to the military, among them *First Blood* (1982), *An Officer and a Gentleman* (1982), *Rambo: First Blood Part II* (1985), and Clancy's string of best-selling "techno-thrillers." The No. 1 box-office draw of 1986, *Top Gun*, showed off sophisticated U.S. military technology—and the bravery and skills of the Navy's elite fighter pilots. Among its many influences, the film caused a run on U.S. Navy ball caps embroidered with the word TOPGUN, and other service-related caps.

Mary Beth Cox, a northern Virginia store owner, says she sold about ten thousand caps in the year after *Top Gun*. "I guess ball caps are a barometer of patriotism," she told the *Washington Post* in 1986. "I think that maybe during Vietnam, which was a bad time, they wouldn't have been as popular."

Cox still sells Navy caps, in addition to caps from all American service branches. While the appeal of military caps has waned since "the *Top Gun* era," she says there is still a steady market for them. "I probably sell about four thousand caps a year now, most of which are military. I carry ball caps from all of the services ... Caps that appeal to our vets are popular: WWII, Korea, Vietnam, Iraq, etc." Her store, Ship's Hatch, also produces custom-made caps for every U.S. Navy ship that ever sailed.

Military caps, which showed support for the United States and its armed forces during an optimistic decade, continue to be a symbol of patriotism and are often worn by veterans.

FACTOR 8
The Rebellion, Backwards and Sideways

But something else was happening in the 1980s. As the ball cap went mainstream, endorsing such American institutions as Major League Baseball and the military, young people adopted the ball cap and endowed it with another meaning altogether: Wearing a cap became a symbol of personal expression and rebellion—particularly when worn backwards; or sideways.

In the popular music world, two movements turned the ball cap this way: hip-hop and grunge.

Hip-hop, or rap, music was born in New York City during the 1970s. As it became more widespread and eclectic in the eighties—particularly after the founding of Def Jam Recordings in 1984—a hip-hop culture took root, which began to influence music, film, television, and fashion.

An offspring of hip-hop known as "gangsta rap" arrived in the late 1980s. Among the pioneers of this style was a Compton, California-based group called N.W.A. Although their music was often banned from radio play, N.W.A. (which stood for Niggaz With Attitude) sold almost ten million CDs in a five-year lifespan (1986–1991). Group members Dr. Dre, Ice Cube, MC Ren, and Easy-E all went on to become top-selling solo artists. N.W.A.'s music and attitude were outrageously violent and politically incorrect, and also very popular. Their outlaw look included black-and-silver Oakland Raiders ball caps. The ball cap became a hip-hop staple by the early nineties and remains so today.

In the Pacific Northwest, meanwhile—about nine hundred and seventy-five miles north of Compton—another musical rebellion was taking shape. In the mid-1980s, an alternative rock music known as grunge was attracting a following in the Seattle area. Grunge incorporated elements of punk rock and heavy metal, but the music had its own unique sensibility, an odd blend of alienation, anger, and apathy. The best-known bands to come out of this underground rock movement, Nirvana and Pearl Jam, were among the top-selling music artists of the 1990s.

The grunge attitude was reflected in what came to be called "grunge fashion." Grunge fashion was really anti-fashion, a reaction against what some saw as the yuppiefication of America during the 1980s. Many bands, and fans, sported a working-class look that

**Wearing a ball cap has become a symbol of personal expression
and even rebellion.**

seemed inspired by Washington state's lumber industry—checkered
shirts, torn trousers, work boots, and baseball caps worn backwards.

Karl Koch, historian for the New Era cap company, says it all had
something to do with irony. "The classic rock bands never wore caps.
Then the MTV generation came along and there was this shift. It was
okay to do things you'd never done before. It was okay to wear a log-
ging uniform on stage and a baseball cap. Everyone was making fun of
things. Everything was ironic all of a sudden."

What made the Ball Cap Revolution unique, and gives it durability, is that it had so many different origins—baseball, patriotism, rebellion, concern about skin cancer. Also, it's a revolution that embraces different generations.

In 1991, the *New York Times* took notice of the Cap Revolution (without specifically calling it that). In a story titled "Far From Home Plate, Baseball Caps Take Over," (July 10), the *Times* noted: "As baseball's All-Star break winds up today, let us put on our thinking caps, with the bills worn frontward, backward, or off to the side, rapper style. Let us ponder why seven out of ten hats made in this country are baseball caps. Why everyone from football and basketball coaches to movie stars and babies wear them. And why the trend shows no sign of peaking."

A FEW WORDS ABOUT GENERATIONS

By the early 1990s, what might have been called the Ball Cap Generation was clearly coming into its own—although, interestingly, no one thought to call it that. Which was sort of odd, considering all of the other names— many of them quite silly—that were bandied about in an attempt to brand people who grew up in the sixties, seventies, and eighties.

"Generation X" was the most widely used generational tag, referring to people born between, approximately, 1964 and 1980. Some thought "Generation X" was too broad a label, though, so social commentator Jonathan Pontell coined the term Generation Jones, a reference to those born between 1954 and 1965. This was the generation that made the word "jones" a popular slang term for craving or addiction in the 1970s (who can forget the song "Basketball Jones"?). When Barack Obama won the American presidency in 2008, some newspapers called him the first Generation X president; but several political writers/commentators noted that he actually belonged to Generation Jones.

Not surprisingly, Generation Y followed Generation X. Gen Y has been defined as children of the Baby Boomer Generation—those born beginning in the late seventies, or early eighties, to the early nineties (although some of these are technically the children of Generation Jones or, if you'd prefer, the older members of Generation X, and in some cases, include members of the MTV Generation). Gen Y has been called the Sandwich Generation, supposedly because so many of them are staying at home well into their twenties (and, evidently, eating sandwiches). It's interesting to note that the Silent Generation (Americans born between approximately 1925 and 1942) was also called the Sandwich Generation, although not for the same reason.

Some folks born in the early nineties are more appropriately considered members of Generation Z than Generation Y. As you can tell, the length of generations is becoming shorter. Generation Z has also been called The New Silent Generation and Generation V (for Virtual). Because Generation Z tends to be tech-savvy, it has also been dubbed Generation C, a reference to computers. People born on Thursday, of any year, are occasionally called the @Y!T%B Generation (just kidding on that last one).

As generations go, the Ball Cap Generation seems to more closely span a real generation than most others. It came of age at a hopeful time in this country, following the more turbulent sixties and seventies.

Which leads to the question: What does it mean that we have become a Ball Cap Nation?

WHAT IT MEANS

What it means is … well, actually, that's sort of a tricky question. In fact, this is a topic that can seem as ambiguous as a Rorschach inkblot. Take your pick. The popularity of the ball cap shows that we're: sporty; sports-obsessed; independent-minded; hip; hillbillies; the country that invented the automobile and the Internet; the country that actually made "(You're) Having My Baby" a No. 1 hit.

At its worst—when worn to show inner-city gang affiliations—the ball cap seems to represent our most divisive, thuggish nature. At its best—when millions wore New York Yankees caps in the wake of 9/11, for instance—the cap represents a collective commitment to a cause, a reaffirmation of human goodness and charity.

We asked a few sociologists what they think about the ball cap trend. They all spoke of a desire for community and also mentioned the growing casualness in our dress and our attitudes over the past three decades.

Gregory Squires, a professor of sociology at George Washington University, said: "It seems to me this has long been a way for people to express their personal identity and connection with something larger than themselves, something that perhaps more of us should do but not necessarily in terms of pro-sports teams.

"Wearing a cap is, in a small way, to express our sense of being part of a larger community. And sports teams have certainly learned how to exploit that identity and sense of community ... Such identity and connections do not come about naturally or randomly. Professional sports has become, among many other things, a sophisticated marketing machine. Sports teams have convinced local media (newspapers, radio, TV) to give them a lot of free publicity. In many ways, teams nurture fan identification with the home team. Making caps and other paraphernalia available, sometimes inexpensively, is an easy way to nurture that identity (and perhaps loyalty) and the bottom line."

The ball cap encompasses two American traits, which together form what could be called the Great American Contradiction—the simultaneous impulses to rebel and to conform. Our country was founded on a declaration of independence and we reinforce themes of individuality and freedom in the best stories that we tell one another. But we also crave conformity, and ritual, as a means of asserting our national identity. Americans love rebelling en masse. We love creating huge events that everyone watches simultaneously, such as the Super Bowl. We love chain restaurants that serve the same meals whether we're in Omaha or Hong Kong, and we flock to movies such as *Spiderman III* and *The Dark Knight* that "shatter" box-office records. Americans love to feel part of some vague, hopeful, shared idea called America, even if we don't quite know what it is anymore. In this sense, the ball cap fits securely on our national noggin, allowing us to feel part of a community of cap-wearers—and, at the same time, to express whatever the hell we want to express with our own individual caps.

POST-REVOLUTION, OR REVOLUTION II

"Independence is a boom market. It's a lifestyle choice,
a state of mind, a backward baseball cap."

– *Manohla Dargis,* The New York Times
(in a 2007 article on the Sundance Film Festival)

We are now in the midst of what might be called the Second Cap Revolution. Travel with me, if you will, to Saginaw, Michigan. The date is November 6, 2006, a Monday. The Saginaw City Council meeting has just convened. Charles Littleton, a twenty-two-year-old Saginaw Valley State University student, is among those in attendance, earning credit for an urban sociology class. Littleton is wearing a Los Angeles Dodgers baseball cap.

At the start of the meeting, Saginaw Mayor Carol Cottrell reminds audience members to remove their hats. When Littleton doesn't do so, a police officer, Doug Stacer, asks him to take off his ball cap. Littleton wants to know why. A short and heated debate ensues, and then a scuffle, involving other officers. Saginaw Police Chief Gerald Cliff's finger is broken and Littleton is Tasered and dragged from the meeting. Littleton is charged with two felony counts and faces six years in prison.

In interviews after the altercation, Littleton is outspoken, saying that his rights were violated when he was asked to remove his cap. "It means more than just a hat," he tells a television reporter. "It's like my crown. It's like asking a king to remove his crown ... If I was a Jewish man—would you ask me to remove my yarmulke? ... A turban? Anything like that? But I guess a Los Angeles Dodgers hat is not a religious symbol. That is secular. You respect your religion, but you don't respect this."

Littleton will later apologize to the council and the felony charges will be reduced to misdemeanors. But the incident reflects the deep-seated feelings about cap-wearing that have permeated some neighborhoods of America's youth culture in recent years.

Over the past decade, many young people have claimed the ball cap as their own, given it a meaning it didn't have twenty years ago, and taken their caps where no cap had gone before—to restaurants, to classrooms, to church. Hip-hop artists and rockers have even written songs about their caps (as we will see in the next chapter). Cap Revolution II may be more limited and short-lived than the first Cap Revolution of the 1980s. But its participants are clearly quite passionate. At the center of both Cap Revolutions has been an unlikely entity—a family-run business based in Buffalo, New York, which started out nearly ninety years ago, making dress hats for men.

3

TOP CAP: THE NEW ERA STORY

How a modest, family-run business became the

world's largest manufacturer of ball caps;

a visit to the New Era cap company in Buffalo;

a conversation with its CEO;

and a tour of its cap factory.

"Now the critics wanna hit it
This hit? How we did it, just because they don't get it
But I'll stay fitted, New Era committed
Now this red cap gets a rap from these critics"
– Fred Durst, Limp Bizkit, from
"Take a Look Around (Theme from Mission Impossible II*)"*

ONE measure of how far the baseball cap has come over the past quarter century is the number of ball caps produced annually by New Era, the world's largest cap maker. In 1982, the Buffalo, New York-based company manufactured 1.4 million baseball caps; in 1989, production had increased to 5.6 million. The growth continued by leaps and bounds: in 1993, New Era made 12.3 million caps; in 2000, 19 million; in 2005, 30.6 million; in 2008, 35 million.

But two barometers that are perhaps even more telling are these: the striking change in

New Era's image over the past decade and the expansion of its international market during that time, from three to forty-seven countries.

Since the late 1990s, when Fred Durst of the rock band Limp Bizkit literally began singing the praises of New Era, the cap producer has taken on a youth culture cachet and street cred that would have seemed unimaginable in the 1960s or '70s. New Era caps, with their side flag logos and flattened brims, are now staples of urban and shopping mall fashion; they're seen—often worn backwards or sideways—in music videos, MTV shows, films, on album covers, even on fashion runways. Many cap buyers leave the silver-dollar-sized New Era stickers on the brims to show that their caps are authentic. More than two dozen entertainers and athletes, from Spike Lee to Ludacris, have designed limited edition New Era cap lines. And in 2006, hip-hop singer Lil' Flip even wrote and recorded an ode to his New Era cap, called "New Era."

If all of this sounds a bit faddish, it may be. But New Era has more going for it than the whims of popular fashion. The company, which makes all of the caps for Major League Baseball, has methodically built a solid market foundation on a number of fronts. A decade ago, New Era did less than two million dollars worth of international business; it now does fifty million, with a growth rate of about 20 percent each year, according to company CEO Christopher Koch. The company recently inked a seven-year deal with Mainland Headwear Holdings, one of Asia's leading distributors and retailers of ball caps, a significant move into the growing Chinese market.

New Era has also diversified in recent years, partnering with other powerhouse companies such as Marvel Comics and DC Shoes, opening flagship retail stores, and producing apparel and other nonbaseball-cap headwear. Overall, company revenues topped $350 million in 2008.

Despite its trendy image and what is sometimes perceived as overnight success, New Era has in fact quietly been making caps for nearly ninety years. A fourth-generation, family-run business, New Era was launched in Buffalo in 1920 by Koch's great grandfather Ehrhardt as a maker of men's dress hats. In the 1930s, it began selling ball caps to professional baseball; baseball caps became the mainstay of its operation after World War II and have been ever since. Starting in 1993, New Era has been the exclusive supplier of caps to Major League Baseball. It also makes the caps worn by about three hundred college and Minor League baseball teams in the United States. Launched in a rented office space in downtown Buffalo, the company today employs about seventeen hundred people worldwide.

Whether New Era has shrewdly reaped the benefits of the world's cap craze or whether it helped to bring about that craze is a good question; probably, it was a combination of both. In search of answers— and to learn more about the company—we journey to New Era's offices and production plant in Buffalo.

CAPS TO RICHES

The New Era story begins with Ehrhardt Koch, whose parents emigrated to New York from Germany in the late 1800s, when Ehrhardt was two, settling in an established German neighborhood on the east side of Buffalo.

In 1902, sixteen-year-old Ehrhardt took his first job, with the Miller Brothers Cap Company of Buffalo, where he began to learn the trade of hat-making. Buffalo was a thriving city then, the eighth largest in the United States. Its rise had begun in 1825 with the opening of the Erie Canal; by the end of the nineteenth century, Buffalo was among the country's top producers of grain and steel. It was also the first city in the country with widespread electric lighting, generated by turbines at nearby Niagara Falls. In 1901, "The City of Light," as Buffalo called itself, hosted the Pan-American Exposition, where it showed off dazzling displays of electric lights to a world still awed by the novelty of electricity. (The most notable event of the exposition, however, was unexpected and tragic: President William McKinley was in a receiving line at the Exposition's Pavilion of Music on September 6 when he was shot by a deranged anarchist; McKinley, six months into his second term, died in Buffalo eight days later; Theodore Roosevelt was sworn in as president, also in Buffalo, early on the afternoon of September 14.)

Ehrhardt stayed with the Miller Brothers company for eighteen years, working his way up to manager of the cutting department—but no further. According to New Era historian Karl Koch, Ehrhardt was frustrated in his attempts to rise higher within the company, and finally became convinced that the only way he would get to the top would be to start at the top, with his own company. At age thirty-four, he talked his aunt into taking out a second mortgage on her house and lending him the five thousand dollars he needed to launch the E. Koch Cap Company. She did so after Ehrhardt assured her he would always provide jobs for her children.

He started his company with fourteen employees, including his sister Rose and Joe Amerien, a fellow worker from Miller Brothers. Ehrhardt set up shop on the third floor of an office building at 1830 Genesee Street, and began to produce men's dress caps, known as Pacer hats—eight-panel wool caps with a short bill and loose crown top—which he sold to men's stores. The company made approximately sixty thousand caps in 1920, and sold them for $3.98 a dozen.

In 1922, Ehrhardt changed the name of the company from E. Koch to New Era. Karl Koch (Ehrhardt's great grandson), who is compiling a history of New Era, says he hasn't been able to find any records explaining exactly why Ehrhardt chose that name. "It seems like a pretty advanced name for the time. But then I looked at other businesses and found that there were several products that used that term, New Era. I'm guessing he saw it on another product and liked the sound of it. I think it probably reflected the mood that people felt in the 1920s. It was a time of optimism."

New Era's caps were not much different from what the larger Miller Brothers Company was selling, but Ehrhardt was determined that his firm stand out for its attention to quality and detail. One of New Era's early mottos was "Quality First, Quantity Will Follow." Ehrhardt believed that if his company produced the best caps on the market, customers would return for more. And they did. Ehrhardt also believed in building his firm on a family foundation. In 1925, his only child Harold joined New Era, and Ehrhardt set out to teach him the ins and outs of the cap business.

Nine years later, with America mired in the Depression, Harold convinced his father to diversify New Era by producing baseball caps. Baseball was thriving at the time, and dress clothing sales were in a slump. Ehrhardt resisted the idea at first, though. According to Karl Koch, "He thought, Why mess with a good formula? Why change what has made us successful? But I think he must've also seen the writing on the wall."

The company's first professional baseball caps were produced in 1934 on a one-year contract—home and away caps for the Cleveland Indians. New Era also began making "private label" caps at about this time for sporting-goods giants Spalding and Wilson, which would attach their labels to the caps and sell them to the pro teams. "That's how most of the caps were sold," Koch says. "The idea of going directly to a club, as they did with Cleveland and would later, must've taken a lot of chutzpah."

There's a recurring pattern in the New Era story, a kind of generational baton-passing in which the company advances not just by outpacing the competition, but also by reinventing the game. In a sense, each generation has done this. It began when Ehrhardt's son Harold steered the company into the ball cap business in the mid 1930s. Over the next two decades, New Era made several key design changes to its baseball caps—notably the fortified crown—that would become part of the pro-ball cap. The company's 59Fifty design, or "Brooklyn"-style cap, introduced in 1954, is the same basic design worn in Major League Baseball today. (59Fifty is a reference to the cap's original catalogue number: 5950. "We probably should come up with a better story to tell people than that," CEO Chris Koch says.)

Harold Koch's son David became the head of the company in 1982. Under his leadership, New Era broadened its reach, increasing sales to college teams, minor leagues, international baseball, the military, and the golf and tennis markets.

One of David Koch's aims was to win the business of all twenty-six teams then in Major League Baseball (the league expanded to twenty-eight teams in 1993, and to thirty teams in 1998), and his efforts finally paid off in 1993, when New Era was granted an exclusive contract to produce MLB caps.

New Era experienced its most striking growth under fourth-generation leader Christopher Koch, who was named president in 1993. When he became CEO in 2002, Koch set a goal of doubling the company's revenues within five years, in large part by expanding New Era's overseas operations; the goal was achieved in about four years, with revenues reaching $250 million. He did so by overlaying an idea onto the company's business strategy that no one had thought was particularly important until the 1990s; or, put another way, by changing the game.

NEW ERA CAP PRODUCTION

1982	1.4 million
1985	2.5 million
1989	5.6 million
1993	12.3 million
2000	19 million
2005	30.6 million
2008	35 million

New Era founder Ehrhardt Koch (center), his son Harold (right), and Edward Mittelberger of Marine Midland Trust Bank of Buffalo.

SELLING THE BRAND

Fifteen years ago, New Era didn't even have a marketing department. When Chris Koch became president in 1993, one of the things he wanted to do was to give New Era a greater profile in the sports apparel marketplace. The company had just won the first-ever exclusive contract with Major League Baseball. At the same time, the popularity of baseball caps was soaring. Most people didn't know the name New Era, though. Players did, but not fans. Koch saw this as a company weakness.

"That's when I said to my father, 'We either have to get bigger or we're going to get smaller,'" he recalls. "It was kind of a funny statement, but the sports industry was taking off then and it was a time when you were starting to see more marketing and sponsorship deals. I knew we'd have to do a lot more business to support that."

A consumer survey confirmed what Koch suspected. Even though New Era was manufacturing all of the caps for Major League Baseball, the general public didn't know that, and didn't know the name New Era the way it did Adidas or Nike or other top-level sports apparel makers. In response, the company decided to redo its logo and to invest in building a brand, "becoming more of a marketing company, not just a manufacturing company."

"We really did it in reverse," Koch says, sitting in his spacious, third-floor office at New Era's downtown Buffalo headquarters. "There are a lot of companies built around marketing and branding where there isn't really a lot of substance to the product. But we had all these years of building quality headwear. We just never told anybody about it. So we decided to let our story be known. And that sort of became my mission: to get our story out there and build a brand."

Much as the previous generations of CEOs had, Chris Koch learned the cap-making business from the ground up. He started working for New Era as a teenager, doing whatever his father wanted him to do. During summer vacations in high school, he would man a sewing machine on the assembly line, learning the steps involved in piecing together a ball cap. "My father's whole mentoring process was designed to get me to understand how caps are manufactured. He was a manufacturing guy, he wasn't a marketing guy. Years ago, that's what we did: We made baseball caps for baseball teams. That was our business. There was no fan or consumer market business."

Koch, who once had aspirations to become an architect, took college night classes after finishing high school. But he never stopped working for the family business, moving through its various divisions, from production to sales.

"The more I learned, the more I realized it was something I wanted to do," he says. "When my father ran the company, he ran it very tight. He didn't have any middle management in place. It was a smaller business and it worked for him. When I took the reins in the nineties, I was able to create the infrastructure for what I saw was coming. I was able to go out and hire a lot of young people who were excited about working hard and growing a business. It was fun."

Since 2002, in particular, Koch has aggressively widened the scope of New Era's operations. As his brother Karl puts it, "He's built bridges to worlds that New Era had nothing to do with ten years ago."

Those bridges include: launching the New Era Cap Europe division in 2003; opening offices in Japan, Hong Kong, Australia, the United Kingdom, Germany, California; starting New Era flagship stores in New York City, Buffalo, Toronto, Berlin, London, Birmingham (England), Atlanta, and Amsterdam; securing contracts with dozens of international sports teams; partnering with Marvel and D.C. Comics to produce limited-edition caps coinciding with film releases including *Iron Man*, *The Dark Knight*, and *The Incredible Hulk*; collaborating with other brands, such as DC Shoes, to create joint product lines—in this case, matching headwear and shoes; selling limited-edition, custom cap lines, some designed by celebrities; vastly expanding the number of cap styles and colors available so that New Era produces "tens of thousands of different caps," according to Koch.

"We call it growing the company in nontraditional ways," he says. "Thinking about the consumers, giving them something new, and looking at other brands that are sort of hot that we might get together with."

In November 2006, New Era made room for the future by moving its corporate headquarters from its cramped facility in Derby, New York, where it shared space with a production plant, to the four-story, former Federal Reserve Building in downtown Buffalo.

New Era's remarkable growth hasn't all gone smoothly. Along the way, not surprisingly, the company has suffered some growing pains and a few reputation-denting controversies, including a prolonged labor dispute and allegations of racial discrimination. In 2001 and 2002, workers at the company's New York plant went on strike for nearly a year and several colleges dropped New Era as their supplier following allegations of poor health and safety conditions, low wages, and unfair quotas. The strike ended in 2002 with New Era and its local union, Communications Workers of America 14177, settling on a four-year contract (in 2005, New Era and CWA 14177 were awarded Cornell University's Champion Award for settling the dispute). More recently, the Teamster's Union and the NAACP accused New Era of discrimination and union-busting at its facility in Mobile, Alabama. In February 2008, after months of conflict, New Era, the Teamsters, and the NAACAP announced an agreement with workers at the Mobile facility. Teamsters President James Hoffa said the new contract would benefit both "New Era workers and the company's growth."

Koch is both a business visionary and a traditionalist, who seems anchored to his community yet anxious to take New Era around the world. The company has weathered its storms and continues to look forward— at new ways of growing and diversifying, including significant expansion into China and throughout Europe. There's talk about opening new flagship stores; of collaborations with high-end fashion brands; of non-headwear apparel, possibly even a line of New Era footwear.

But there's a conservative philosophy keeping hold of these ambitions, which Koch says ties today's New Era back to the firm that Ehrhardt Koch founded in 1920. "We can grow in all sorts of other directions, but at the end of the day we're a headwear company and we never want to hurt that. Sometimes people grow so much that they lose sight of what they are. We've become what we are because we produce a quality headwear product and we don't want to forget that."

New Era's contract with Major League Baseball is today about half of the company's business—not in terms of actual on-field caps produced; in terms of the licensing of authentic caps, which are produced in thousands of different styles. The MLB licensing deal comes up for renewal again in 2014. A Request for Proposal will be announced then and most of the large sports apparel suppliers, and many smaller ones, will respond. Is Koch concerned that the company's largest customer could be taken away?

"People ask that," he says. "'Aren't you worried that someone will come along and buy the business?' The only thing I can say is that if it really just came down to money in the end, I guess we could lose it. We can't compete against a fifteen-billion-dollar company. I think we're uniquely positioned because of the number of years we've been doing this and the service we give to baseball. We service the league, the consumers, the teams, right down to the clubhouse level. We're always trying to do the right thing for Major League Baseball. That's our heritage. So I feel confident."

Another question he's sometimes asked is whether he expects a fifth generation of the Koch family will be handed the New Era baton; and, if so, where they might take it. Koch says it's too early to say. He has a son and a daughter, both in their early twenties, and also a nine-month-old baby. "My older children are designers," he says. "Neither of them is technically in the business. They're doing their own thing right now. Which is fine. What I did was hard."

Koch frequently receives overtures from business people wanting to buy New Era. He says he's not interested. "There certainly have been opportunities, but there's really no reason to do it," he says. "I love what I do. I love getting up in the morning and coming in to work. If I sold New Era, I'd have more money, but so what? I'd probably have to go and start something else. I don't want to play golf every day."

SECRETS OF SUCCESS

According to New Era CEO Chris Koch, three elements are behind New Era becoming the world's largest licensed ball cap maker. These are the "secrets" of New Era's success:

1. QUALITY CONTROL. *"This was what the company was founded on, which goes back to my great grandfather. He said that if you make a quality product, you'll get repeat business. There are two parts to that, though. One, obviously, is you produce a good quality product. Two is you have to stay relevant, producing something that the public wants. It's the idea that what was good enough yesterday isn't good enough today. We continue to push that, and drive it through our organization."*

2. AUTHENTICITY. *"Because of the quality of the product, we were able to approach Major League Baseball and convince them that we would service them better than any other company. Making the caps for Major League Baseball gave us authenticity. Major League Baseball is the only sport in the world where headwear is part of the game. And it's part of a game that is America's pastime. We've been making caps for Major League Baseball now for more than seventy years, and that gives us something other companies don't have."*

3. BRANDING. *"New Era means something to people. The name means something. 59Fifty means something. People trust the brand …. The brand gives you something else, even beyond quality. I'm sure if they wanted to, another company could come along and do reverse engineering—they could tear the 59Fifty cap apart, figure out how to make it, and make a similar cap. But it's not going to be a 59Fifty."*

Then-New Era CEO David Koch with sons Christopher and Glen in 1993, the year New Era became the only provider of MLB caps.

THE TWENTY-TWO STEPS

About twenty miles southwest of Buffalo, by the shores of Lake Erie, is the hamlet of Derby, New York, where New Era has maintained a production facility since the early 1960s.

As part of its agreement with Major League Baseball, New Era produces all of its authentic and custom licensed caps in the United States (New Era does outsource about half of its overall cap manufacturing to China, Vietnam, and elsewhere).

On a late-summer morning, the 100,300-square-foot Derby plant hums with the sounds of sewing machines, computer-controlled embroidering drills, and a variety of other machinery. Some three-hundred-and-fifty people work here, in three shifts (midnight to 7 a.m.; 7 a.m. to 3:30 p.m.; and 3:30 p.m. to midnight), producing about seventy-two-thousand caps weekly. New Era also has two manufacturing plants in Alabama, in Jackson and Demopolis, along with a distribution center in Mobile, which employ 362, 405, and 120 respectively.

Robin Thrun, the plant's quality assurance supervisor, and New Era Corporate Communications Manager Dana Marciniak lead three guests on a tour through the Derby facility, showing us the twenty-two steps required to make a New Era ball cap. We're permitted to take photos each step of the way—except, that is, for Step Twenty, which is New Era's guarded process of blocking and steaming the caps into their final shape.

Fellow tour-takers are a female journalist from New York, who is shooting photos of the plant for a magazine story, and Daisuke Fukumori, a brand manager from New Era Cap Japan, who is visiting for several days from Tokyo. We are all struck by how much of the assembly line work is done by hand, by employees sitting in front of sewing machines, attaching panels, sweatbands, and peaks, and by how fast and efficiently the process works.

"If we were to walk straight through, we could make a cap in less than half an hour," says Thrun, who has worked here since 1982. "But each step is done in bunches."

Here, roughly, is how a New Era cap is made:

We begin in the cutting room, where rolls of fabric are piled against the walls. The fabric rolls are unspooled through a layout machine, which cuts the material into the shapes of panel and visor pieces. The cut fabric is then banded and passed on to the next station. The front and back seams of the crown are sewn together on sewing machines and then a tape is applied to the seams, covering the exposed edges of the fabric. Meanwhile, pieces of buckram, the stiffening agent in the crown, are sewn together. Visor panels are joined and a pre-cut visor board is inserted. Next, a closing stitch is applied, creating a finished brim. All of these steps are done by hand. The next few are automated: The peak is placed in a "panagram," which sews decorative

Shelves of caps at the New Era flagship store in Buffalo, New York.

stitches across the brim. Logos are added onto the crown of the cap, with foam applied to give the logo a raised look. The buckram is then bonded and centered to the front panels of the cap. An operator punches holes in the center of each panel of the crown. Middle panels are attached to the front and back panels and the crown is complete. Tape is applied, labels are attached. The peak is then fused onto the brim. A sweatband is sewn inside the cap and licensing labels are attached. Then a "top-stitch" is applied, to hold the crown and sweatband together. Buttons are punched into the top of the crown, joining the seams. Next comes Step Twenty. Then Step Twenty-One, which is inspecting the caps for potential defects, adding visor stickers, and packing them in boxes. "Step Twenty-Two" isn't really a step. It's just the finished cap. (But who's counting?)

NEW ERA ODDS AND ENDS

Most popular cap color: Navy

Color of thread most often used: White

Yards of fabric used to make New Era caps in the
U.S. each year: 2.2 million

Most complex MLB logo: Seattle Mariners

HIP CAP

"Rock it to the front,

Rock it to the back,

I'm so cool wit it in my baseball hat

I keep my fitted real low, low,

New Era,

I keep my fitted real low, low,

New Era."

- Lil' Flip, "New Era"

"We don't pay people to wear our products. They wear them because they
want to. That's sort of the fun part of it."
- New Era CEO Christopher Koch

In 1996, Chris Koch received a call from filmmaker Spike Lee. At
first, he says, he thought it was one of his friends playing a joke. "The
receptionist said Spike Lee's on the phone," he recalls. "I thought,
Okay. He said 'Chris, it's Spike.' I hadn't met him before. He just
cold-called me and he said he wanted us to make him a red Yankees
cap. I remember saying to him, 'Why?' and he said 'Because no one
else has one.'"

Koch made him Yankees caps in six or seven colors, he recalls.
"He thanked me and said, 'That's very nice of you to make me all

those colors. But I'm only going to wear the red one.' I don't think he thought he was starting anything."

The Yankees went to the World Series that year, and they won. Spike Lee, seen on television in his red Yankees cap, sparked an interest in off-color team caps, which were not then available commercially. A few years later, Fred Durst, of the band Limp Bizkit, took to wearing a red New Era Yankees cap onstage when he performed. "That's when it really started to take off," Koch says. Durst sang about his "fitted New Era" cap in the theme song to the movie *Mission Impossible II*. In 2002, he teamed up with the cap company to design a line called Flawless, named after his record label.

The New Era cap was by this time becoming standard apparel in hip-hop culture, worn by artists such as Usher, Ludacris, and Fat Joe. In 2004, New Era launched its "Capture the Flag" series of custom caps, created by some of the top names in hip-hop music. Ludacris, for example, designed a black-and-red cap with a large Atlanta Braves "A," made of clear and black crystals, off to one side, a "Disturbing Tha Peace" logo in the lining, and a "Just Getting Started" logo on back. New Era caps have been worn in hundreds of music videos over the past decade and were a staple on the top-rated MTV program *Rob and Big*.

Fifteen years after Chris Koch set out to build the brand, to create name recognition for his family business, New Era is not only a name that people know; it is also the hippest cap in the land. "Part of it was organic," says Koch, when asked why it happened. "But I also think we've given consumers an opportunity they didn't have before. I mean, how many navy-blue Yankee caps do you want? People wanted the opportunity to go out there and buy caps in any color, combination, or style, and we've made that possible. One thing that's different with us is we'll make very small editions of a highly customized product. A store can order thirty pieces any way they want. That's what happened in the boutique shops in a lot of urban areas, and it caught on."

Top: New Era CEO Christopher Koch, at his office in downtown Buffalo. Center: The Derby plant employs 350 workers who produce about 3.5 million caps per year. Bottom: Team logos are automatically sewn into the front of the cap's crown at New Era's Derby plant.

Koch is a man who obviously enjoys what he's doing. When he got married in 2007, he hired DJ AM to perform at his wedding. "You turn on the TV and see your product, whether it's a sporting event or an entertainment event or a fashion show in Europe. That's satisfying ... It's neat to go down to the locker room at a Yankees game and see the players and talk with them. It's interesting to go to events I wouldn't otherwise get to go to. Like Michael Jordan's party at the NBA All-Star Game. I have fun with it."

And yet, because New Era has become so fashionable so quickly, isn't it possible that the bubble could burst and that New Era—or, more generally, ball caps—could go out of fashion? "I really think it's beyond a fad," Koch says. "Everybody wears caps now and I don't see that changing. It's become a part of America. But again, you've got to work to stay relevant. That's something we take very seriously. As long as we can stay relevant, continue to make a quality product, continue to have the on-field presence with Major League Baseball, I think we'll be around for a long time."

4

THE WILD WORLD OF CAPS

From vintage to propeller-topped
to organic to "trucker" mesh to leather to
garment-washed to gold-topped $2,000 designer
—there's a ball cap for everyone.

ONCE the ball cap caught on, the American imagination took over, creating a market with barely discernable boundaries. Soon, ball caps were being produced in a spectrum of styles, colors, materials, and price ranges. And it wasn't just an American market anymore.

Here is a sampling of some of the ball caps now available: leather caps; organic ball caps; genuine fur ball caps; formal wedding caps (one says "Bride," the other "Groom"); ball caps bearing the flags of each of the world's countries; a thousand-dollar snake-skin cap; an "anatomically correct brain baseball cap"; a "golf ball" cap featuring an artificial turf upper bill with a golf ball attached; covert "spy camera" caps; a cap with a small, solar-powered fan on the brim; caps with front and back bills; Christian ball caps;

Buddhist ball caps; promotional caps advertising everything from beach resorts to sports bras; can-opener caps; a $1,900 cap with a gold button on top; authentic vintage baseball caps; caps with propellers; caps that light up; wooden ball caps; caps with stereo speakers; and many others.

By all accounts, the cap industry has diversified enormously in the past decade, catering to a highly individualized customer base. The Sportsman Cap Network, for instance, a pioneering cap company that has been making and selling caps since 1935, reportedly doubled the size of its catalogue in 2006 to accommodate the specialization of cap tastes.

We decided to venture out into the Wild World of Caps, in search of the more interesting and unusual caps and trends on the market. Here's some of what we found:

FASHION CAPS

The world of fashion is, by definition, a place that often changes. That it would find a spot for the baseball cap is not so surprising; what's surprising is that the ball cap has been there for so long.

Several of the top fashion brands carry designer cap lines. Gucci, for instance, makes a canvas baseball cap that sells for about $225. Prada's nylon ball cap goes for about $285, while Christian Dior produces caps that retail for around $200.

But stylish caps come in many other varieties as well, at prices ranging from twenty or thirty dollars up to, yes, ten thousand dollars.

"Ball caps are extremely fashionable and have been for some time," Ellen Goldstein, chair of Accessories for the Fashion Institute of Technology in New York, told us. "Caps transcend gender. They're not obtrusive, they're not abrasive. They're an icon."

Over the past fifteen years, she says, the ball cap has become an accepted part of American fashion. Goldstein has worn ball caps herself for about twenty-five years. "It's so commonplace now that you don't bat an eye."

One businessman who has tapped into the high-end cap market is Robert Potochnik, who started a luxury headwear company called Zerino several years ago. Potochnik believes that the cap market is due to go the way of luxury cars and luxury watches. "Our customers are proving that there is a market for luxury caps. They're not mainstream, but neither is Rolls Royce or Ferrari," he says.

Potochnik has created a new level of luxury cap, with silk linings, hand-stitching, twenty-two-karat gold top buttons, and detailing reminiscent of other designer fashions. Zerino's caps range from eighty-nine to two thousand dollars (the company's website is www.zerino.com), although they will also make a customized cap for ten thousand dollars, he says, which is "custom-fitted and designed ... like a finely tailored suit."

Goldstein, on the other hand, maintains that a cap can be fashionable without being expensive. Although she works in the world of fashion, she never wears a cap that costs more than forty or fifty dollars, she says. "I'm a New York Giants fan. I especially like to wear my Giants cap."

GEEK HERITAGE

As a kind of homage to the once nerdy image of the baseball cap, Bruce Evans sells a mix of ball caps—including some with propellers—at a website he calls GeekCulture.com.

In the age of Bill Gates, a perceptual shift has occurred in America, and what was once considered nerdy is now sort of cool—or, to paraphrase Gordon Gekko in the film *Wall Street*, "Geek is good." That's the general idea behind GeekCulture, which was created ten years ago by Evans and Liza Schmalcel (their online names are Snaggy and Nitrozac). It's a techno humor site, online community, and web store, with a distinctly geeky point of view. In addition to such items as Steve Jobs and Steve Wozniak buttons, Bill Gates water globes, and "Geekier Than Thou" T-shirts, the website store sells traditional ball caps and brim-less

GeekCulture founders Bruce Evans and Liza Schmalcel
(aka Snaggy and Nitrozac).

beanie propeller caps. But it also gives cap buyers the option of adding
one, two, or three propellers to a standard baseball cap.

Evans, whose self-bestowed titles include "Chief Propeller Beanie
Technician," also writes a comic strip, which, like the website, lov-
ingly pokes fun at the world of technology and computer geeks. Based
in Vancouver, British Columbia, Evans calls his business "Canada's
largest exporter of propeller beanies," and notes that he does all of his
own propeller work. But he isn't the only source of propeller beanies or propeller ball caps. In fact, the market for these has grown surprisingly large.

The propeller beanie was purportedly invented by science-fiction
writer and cartoonist Ray Nelson in 1947 when he was in high
school. On his website, Nelson says that the propeller beanie will
most likely outlive his other work: "Centuries after all my writings

have been forgotten, in some far corner of the galaxy, a beanie-copter will still be spinning."

With the 1962 cartoon show *Beany and Cecil*—in which Beany's propeller cap actually enabled him to lift off the ground and fly—propeller caps briefly became a popular novelty item. But they soon went the way of the Davy Crockett coonskin cap (although science-fiction fans would sometimes create their own beanie caps and wear them at sci-fi conventions). With the rise of computer nerds in the 1990s, the propeller beanie enjoyed a resurgence, becoming a symbol of geekdom. It was perhaps inevitable that ball caps and propellers would eventually get together.

But who buys and wears propeller caps? We spoke with Evans about geeks and propellers.

BCN: What is the "geek culture" philosophy, if it can be put into words?
BE: Everyone has his or her own definition of it. But, for us, it is to keep exploring and keep learning, and to not be afraid to be an individual.

BCN: Propeller ball caps definitely convey "geek." But aren't ball caps considered sort of hip these days?
BE: Yes, ball caps have been hip for a while. Of course, it's hip to be a geek now.

BCN: On what occasions do people wear propeller caps?
BE: People wear them when they want to get some attention. At a party, for instance, or even in a bar (it's one way of "gaming" a girl, striking up a conversion with her). Mostly, they are seen as a sign of respect for a geek, given to or worn by someone who has excelled in his or her field. Often, people will literally "put on the propeller beanie" while working on a tough assignment—coding, for instance—for inspiration. They're also especially popular at trade shows and sporting events. They draw attention to the wearer and lighten up the moment.

BCN: Where did the Geek Culture idea come from?

BE: It actually started as a project to make an interactive DVD about astronauts and the moon. But we soon realized that we were much more interested in the geeks behind the control panels at Mission Control than in the astronauts.

VINTAGE CAPS

In the rolling hills outside of Cooperstown, New York, Will Arlt produces vintage baseball caps—authentic reproductions of the caps worn by major and minor league teams dating back to the mid-1800s. His thirty-page catalogue features illustrations of more than two thousand cap styles, among them the caps worn by every Major League Baseball team, along with Minor League teams, Negro League teams, Mexican and Cuban teams, even prison teams.

If you want a vintage cap that isn't in Arlt's catalogue, it doesn't matter. He takes special orders, researching the requested item through old catalogues, photographs, and museum archives, and re-creates the cap in its original style, using the same materials as in the original.

Arlt started his business, the Cooperstown Ball Cap Company (www.ballcap.com), twenty years ago because he saw a need that no one was filling. "Many people have a favorite baseball team that they grew up with. The team maybe doesn't exist anymore or the uniform has changed. But it still means something to them. I provide a service ... There are very few things made in America anymore that are identical to what existed fifty or seventy years ago. We're kind of going against that idea."

He discusses his business over lunch in Cooperstown, a village steeped in baseball lore, where the storefronts along Main Street have such names as Extra Innings, Mickey's Place, Doubleday Café, The On Deck Circle, Triple Play Café, Safe at Home, and Seventh Inning Stretch.

Arlt grew up worlds away from this bucolic lakeside village, in

Vintage cap maker Will Arlt on Main Street, Cooperstown, New York.

Brooklyn, New York. He studied philosophy in college and worked for a time as an engineer with Atlantic Records, on albums by Iron Butterfly, Aretha Franklin, the Young Rascals, and others. In the early seventies, he was part of an "underground" musical ensemble called the People's Victory Orchestra and Chorus, which still has a very small cult following. "Then the yuppies came in and the underground disappeared," he says.

Arlt wanted to do something on his own, something no one else was doing. During a visit to Cooperstown in 1982 he had a Eureka moment. Walking through the National Baseball Hall of Fame, Arlt saw a blue-and-gray Walter Johnson Washington Senators cap—and it rekindled something, he says, reminding him of the caps of his youth and the magic of baseball.

He began to study caps. "I'd look for old woolen caps and then alter them to make them seem vintage—open them up, cut down the length of the brim, and hand-embroider a logo. No one was making vintage caps at the time."

Arlt was able to sell a few of those; but, he says, "They were all grimy and sweaty. So, at a certain point, I said, 'Let me see if I can make this from scratch.'"

In 1988, he moved to a farm outside Cooperstown and started his cap company. At first, he cut and sewed the caps himself, by hand, spending about six hours on each. His business was mail-order and grew largely by word of mouth. During his first year, he managed to sell about five hundred caps. "Who anticipates one's life?" he says. "You do something and if it works, you keep doing it."

In June of 1989, *Sports Illustrated* ran a story about Arlt. "Four days later, there was three thousand dollars in the mail, from all these people wanting old caps. That's when I had to get serious."

People wanted vintage ball caps, more than he had imagined. They still do. In a sense, Arlt is a nostalgia merchant. He makes caps for people who want to connect with their pasts, with some deep-rooted feelings connected with baseball. Arlt knows about that. He grew up following the Brooklyn Dodgers, in the days of Jackie Robinson and Duke Snider. He used to save the tops of ice cream cups and redeem them for tickets to see the Dodgers at Ebbets Field. He played baseball himself as a boy and later pitched for the Cooperstown ABCs, a vintage ball team that plays barehanded, as teams did in the 1800s.

"There's something pastoral and ethereal about baseball that is not attained by other sports," Arlt says. "Baseball has a history that precedes the Civil War. It's part of the American fabric."

Arlt's catalogue isn't only a listing of products; it also charts the changes in each team's ball caps through the years, including home and away caps, beginning with the Brooklyn Excelsiors in 1860. "That catalogue, and the website," he says, "are a lifetime of work." Along the way, Arlt got to know the history of Major League ball caps probably as well as anyone. "You see how they gradually changed," he says. "It was a long, gradual process. When we make a cap from 1901 or 1902, you can ball it up and put it in your pocket because the visors were so flexible back then. They were made of cardboard."

Because Arlt sells to a niche buyer, his business hasn't been affected much by the ball cap boom of the past decade. "To buy my caps, you have to be interested in baseball," he says. He's been selling about five thousand caps a year since the mid-nineties. Some are sold to teams, most to individuals. His clients have included costumers for several baseball movies, including *The Babe* and *A League of Their Own*. The late comedian George Carlin used to buy caps from him, he says (all with either a "G" or a "C" on the crown).

A few years after Arlt started his business, a San Francisco company called Blue Marlin began selling vintage caps in styles commemorating Negro League, Latin League, and Minor League teams. The company, founded in 1994 by former investment banker Erik Stuebe and designer Francoise Sejourne, won an avid following. Its soft, thick-brushed cotton caps were sold in limited editions in Bloomingdales and other high-end stores. When celebrities such as Bruce Willis, Bruce Springsteen, Cindy Crawford, and Brad Pitt began wearing them, Blue Marlin became, for a few years, one of the trendiest ball caps. Blue Marlin has since developed an extensive sportswear line. It continues to sell vintage ball caps, but they are now only a small part of the company's business.

Arlt, on the other hand, has stuck with his vintage caps, which he still often sells one at a time. "I'm content," he says, "to keep the house standing, make some baseball caps, read philosophy …. This isn't a business where you make a lot of money; it's a business that provides a service. That's what I do."

The All-American Girls' Baseball Leauge of the 1940s was the inspiration for the movie *A League of Their Own,* **one of the baseball movies using caps designed by Will Arlt.**

Arlt doesn't make the caps himself any more. The production is overseen by his head seamstress, Susan Whitmore. He says he sometimes wonders what will happen to the business after she retires. Arlt has a son, but says he isn't especially interested in vintage ball caps. "I'll do it as long as I can. If I could find a young buck who was passionate for baseball and wanted to take over, I would transfer it to him. But you don't find that much any more. People want to mass produce everything."

In the meantime, Arlt feels a responsibility to his customers. "There are some business people who don't consider who's on the other end of what they're producing," he says. "I know someone who had a restaurant that a lot of people liked. But he decided he would open another place and he closed the restaurant. When he did that, he was removing something that meant a lot to people. He felt that because he owned the restaurant, he could do that. I don't know that you can. I'm interdependent on the people I serve."

FREEDOM OF CHOICE

Fred Belinsky got into the ball cap game after what he calls "that fateful spring" of 1981. When he started his Village Hat Shop in San Diego in 1980, Belinsky was selling primarily Western hats. The John Travolta-Debra Winger film *Urban Cowboy* had just come out and the country was in the midst of a neo-cowboy craze.

But the mood changed starkly in the spring of 1981. "People in the headwear industry still talk about it," he says. "The Western craze just suddenly stopped. All of a sudden, the jobbers had warehouses filled with cowboy hats and no one wanted them."

The change began a decade-long period when licensed ball caps were his bread-and-butter business. Then, when retail specialists such as Lids and Hat World came along in the 1990s, Belinsky's focus shifted again. More recently, Indiana Jones-style hats and fedoras have been his big sellers. But the Village Hat Shop—which in 1997 became one of the first hat retailers to go online—sells a little of everything, from berets to Ivy caps to top hats.

Belinsky has observed many trends in the hat industry over the past thirty years. "Our strength," he says, "has been our ability to move quickly and respond to whatever is going on in headwear." The Village Hat Shop now has four stores in California and is one of the largest online hat operations. Its website (villagehatshop.com) is also a lively source of information on the history of hats and caps (listings include "Hats in Art" and "Hats and Children's Literature").

A big change in the cap industry came in the 1980s, Belinsky says, with the widespread availability of heat transfer imprint machines. "That changed the business. It suddenly became inexpensive and easy to make personalized caps," he says.

Belinsky recalls creating a brochure that advertised "Walking Billboards."

"That was my marketing catch. I encouraged people, if they had a plumbing business or a ball team or a family reunion, they could come in and get six, twelve, or twenty-four hats."

Custom-designed caps continue to be a healthy segment of the cap market. Belinsky, who points out that the baseball cap is the only truly American hat (cowboy hats probably originated in Spain), says there is something very American about being able to design your own ball cap. "It's an American idea, a perfect fit for a country that glorifies democracy," he says.

FRIEDLANDER CAPS

Speaking of custom caps: If you've seen television's *30 Rock*, you've seen some of Judah Friedlander's ball caps. Judah plays Frank Rossitano, a television writer, on the show. Frank is never seen without a trucker-style cap bearing a personalized, often cryptic, message. His caps, which aren't talked about on the show, provide a running, deadpan parody of pop culture slogans. Here are a few of his cap sayings: "Feelin It," "UFO Cop," "Bigfoot Expert," "Phase 3," "Alabama Legsweep," "Karate Sluts," "Time

Travel Agent," "Squeeze It," "Cool As Ice," and "Extra Cheese."

The caps were Friedlander's idea, not Frank Rossitano's. "I make all the caps myself," Friedlander tells us. "I have been making my own caps for about fifteen years."

TRUCKER CAPS

"I looked at the company. There were two young farmer boys from North
Dakota in red baseball caps, which is the standard
North Dakota farmer boy hat ..."
– *Jack Kerouac,* On the Road, *published in 1957*

In an earlier incarnation, farmer and trucker caps were given away at grain stores and farm equipment dealerships (see Chapter 2). They were worn by workers and truck drivers to shield the sun from their eyes. When the caps became grimy after a few weeks or months, the wearers would replace them. Few people thought to save these caps.

As sometimes happens in our country, though, time has added value to a product we once took for granted. The trucker cap—which has an ancestral lineage very different from that of the baseball cap— is now seen as emblematic of the American heartland, of working-class values, of Made-in-the-U.S.A. production. It represents America, but with an emphasis on labor and industry, rather than sports.

This idea, percolating for years, went mainstream with the recent endorsements by high-profile trucker-cap wearers such as Ashton Kutcher, Johnny Knoxville, and Christina Aguilera. Kutcher, in fact, is sometimes credited with single-handedly changing the image of the trucker cap—although in 2008, singer Justin Timberlake took issue with this perception, telling a fashion magazine that he has worn trucker caps since he was seventeen.

Whatever the reason—and wherever the credit is due—caps advertising John Deere or Caterpillar or Mack are no longer "gimme caps," as the trucker hats used to be called. They're pure Americana now.

A British company called Capitate bills itself as "The U.K.'s Biggest and Best Website for Authentic Trucker Hats," including Peterbilt, John Deere, and Von Dutch. "At Capitate," its website says, "you'll only find trucker hats worn by truckers. We have hooked up with American truck manufacturer Mack to bring you the coolest looking mesh-back mother truckin' baseball caps on the market."

COMFORT CAPS

An ongoing cap trend is the desire for ball caps that appear old but are actually new—caps with a washed-out, worn-in look. Twins Enterprise, a popular Massachusetts cap-maker, specializes in what are called garment-washed and distressed-fabric cotton caps. These are caps that have been air-washed, sandblasted, and in some cases deliberately torn or frayed. The idea is to create the look and feel of a "favorite hat" that is several years old, says a spokesman for the company.

Call them Comfort Caps. For many cap-wearers, comfort is what really matters. Take President Obama. After his election victory on November 4, 2008, Obama wore an old Chicago White Sox cap every time he went out in public. In Hawaii, he was photographed wearing the cap backwards. It was apparently the same cap that Obama had worn earlier in the year. When he was pictured wearing it during the campaign, White Sox Chairman Jerry Reinsdorf asked Scott Reifert, the Sox's vice president of communications, to provide Obama with two brand-new White Sox caps. He did. But Obama continued to wear the worn-in cap. "I've never seen the two new caps," Reifert told the *Chicago Tribune*. "I don't think he ever wore them."

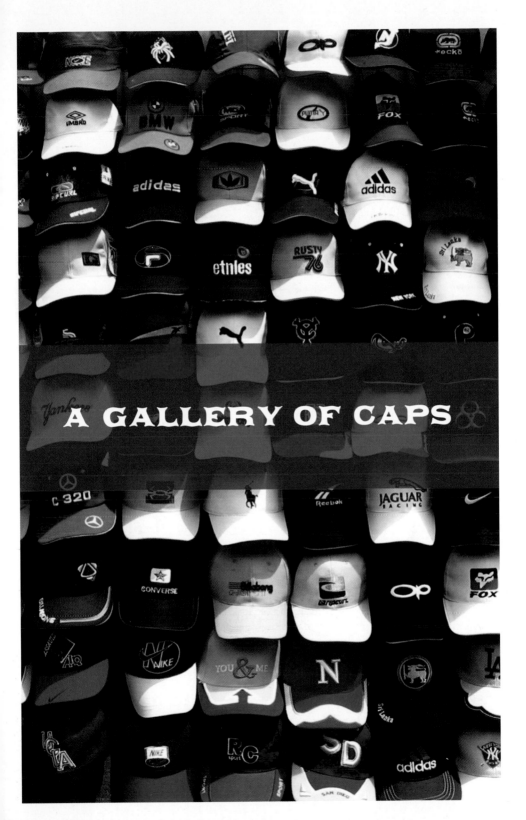

A GALLERY OF CAPS

Opening page: An assortment of ball caps for sale from a street vendor in Sri Lanka.
Left: President Obama wearing his favorite White Sox cap. Above: The Dalai Lama sported
a Washington Nationals baseball cap during his recent visit to the nation's capital.

Top: Guinness Book record-holder Buckey Legried with some of his more than 90,000 ball caps, at home in Frost, Minnesota. Above, left: Here comes the bride's ball cap, from a Las Vegas wedding chapel. Above, right: The ball cap has become a fashion icon, according to one fashion expert.

Pioneering cap wearer Spike Lee, wearing a Brooklyn cap.
The filmmaker helped popularize MLB caps in non-team colors.

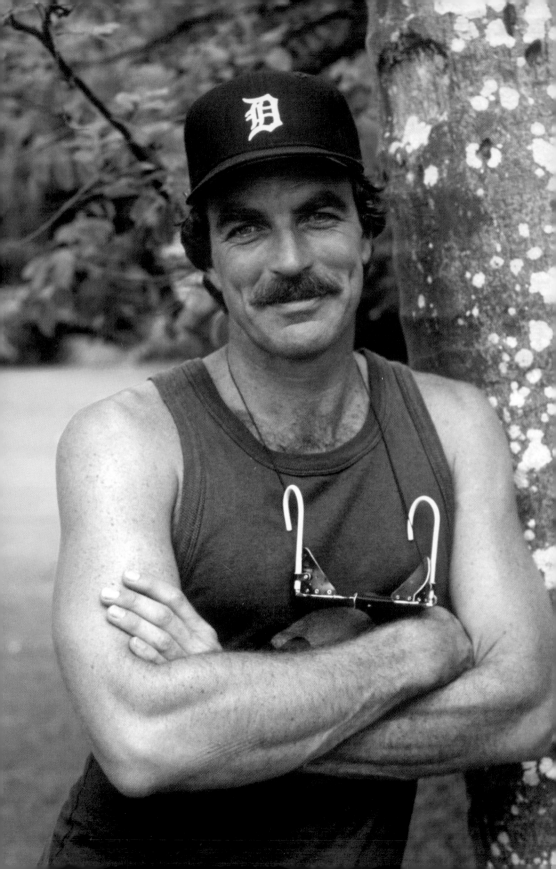

Left: Tom Selleck as Magnum, P.I., the first hero/sex symbol known for wearing a baseball cap. Above: Children in the Democratic Republic of Congo, many of whom had never before worn new clothing, happy with their Super Bowl caps.

Judah Friedlander of television's *30 Rock* and a few of his custom-made caps.

THE NEXT WAVE

With advances in technology, the baseball cap is bound to see some evolutionary changes in the months and years ahead. Will the public support these changes, or will it always prefer the simplicity of the basic baseball cap? We tried a few of the latest cap innovations on for size.

Air Conditioned Caps

True air-conditioned ball caps have not yet arrived—although several versions of the solar-powered fan cap are on the market. The standard fan cap features a small plastic fan inserted in the bill of the cap and a solar panel on top of the crown. The solar panel provides the power to turn the fan blades, which spin air into the wearer's face. When used indoors or on cloudy days, the fan may also be operated by batteries. Clip-on fans are also available, which attach to the brim of the cap. If nothing else, cap fans are a sure way to inspire smiles and double-takes when worn in public.

Hidden Camera Caps

Spy culture has piggybacked on the country's cap craze by producing hidden camera caps, also known as "covert caps." These typically feature a small video camera in the lining of the cap's crown, which captures images through a pinhole-size lens in the front logo and transmits them to a wireless receiver.

There are several different spy cap cameras for sale on the Internet, ranging in price from about two hundred dollars to more than twelve hundred dollars.

"Trying to catch the culprit? You won't strike out again with our baseball cap wireless hidden camera," teases one website. "Great to wear for up-close surveillance or almost any covert operation."

The ad also points out, correctly, "It is the customer's responsibility to use their camera in accordance with all state and federal government laws."

These spy-cams come with both black-and-white and color cameras. Some contain "audio modules."

We conducted a covert operation to determine which of these hidden cap cameras works the best. The mission was completed shortly before this book went to press. A 347-page report is pending approval of the publisher and the House Intelligence Committee. (The results will be classified.)

Organic Caps

As the demand for environmentally sensitive products heightens, organic caps are increasingly popular. These are caps made from organic cotton, meaning cotton grown without pesticides and not genetically modified. In 2007, 265,517 bales of organic cotton were produced around the world, according to *The Organic Exchange Organic Farm and Fiber Report 2007*. The largest producers were Turkey, India, and China. The United States ranked ninth, out of the twenty-four nations listed.

Although they look and behave much like non-organic cotton caps, organic caps sometimes have a softer feel and, according to one organic cap-maker, "They give you a good feeling inside, too."

In 2009, Twins Enterprise began selling licensed recycled baseball caps, made in part from recycled plastic. Numerous other cap manufacturers have introduced "green" lines in the past several years. Expect much more to come.

Head Lights

The idea of "hat lights" very nearly makes sense. If you're going out at night on your bicycle or in your automobile, after all, you would be sure to turn on your lights. So why not have lights on your cap, too, for when you take it out after dark?

Several companies have turned this notion into a product—what's known in the industry as "LED caps." These are caps that contain a light, or several lights, attached to the brim, which shine in whichever direction the cap is pointed (this can be a problem, of course, for those who prefer to wear their caps backwards).

One online LED cap ad calls it "extremely useful" for "general house repairs, night fishing, looking cool, or avoiding the muddy bits in the field on the way back from the pub" (yes, this is a British version).

(LED, for those who were wondering, is short for "light-emitting diode," which, according to Wikipedia, is "a semiconductor device that emits incoherent narrow-spectrum light when electrically biased in a forward direction of the p-n junction." Those same words, of course, have also been used on occasion to describe our country's foreign policy.)

Damn Seagulls, Etc.

With all of these sophisticated new ball caps coming onto the market, some folks are probably wondering, "Hey, what about the good old novelty cap?" You know, like the cap with plastic dog poop on the brim. Or those mesh caps with clever sayings, like, "I Used to Have a Handle On Life But It Broke"; "I'm a Senior Citizen: Now Gimme a Discount"; "Do Not Disturb (I'm Disturbed Enough)"; "Jesus Is Coming (Act Busy)"; "I Used to Be Schizophrenic But Now We're Fine."

Perhaps the most quintessential novelty caps were the ones with the words "Damn Seagulls," splotched with what were supposed to be seagull droppings. They were sometimes tailored to individual coastal markets in the United States, Canada, and elsewhere. On Prince Edward Island, for instance, you could purchase a cap that read, "Damn Those Prince Edward Island Seagulls."

Fortunately, you can still find that cap on Prince Edward Island—and similar versions in other coastal locales. Yes, in a world where high-end ball caps sell for up to ten thousand dollars, it's refreshing to know that novelty caps are not an endangered species.

THE FUTURE

Where is this Wild World of Caps ultimately leading us? What does cap technology hold in store: Interactive caps capable of talking with us? Caps that answer the telephone? That speak German? That yodel? That drive? That scream when we behave like idiots?

These scenarios are not as far-fetched as they may seem (except for that one about yodeling). In fact, a team of researchers in Taiwan has designed a ball cap that is able to detect and analyze electrical activity in the brain. Their project, reported by the Institute of Electrical and Electronics Engineers, Inc. (IEEE), involves what is known as a brain computer interface (BCI). The cap contains five electrodes that attach to the wearer's forehead, and one electrode that attaches behind the left ear, which collect electro-encephalography (EEG) signals. These signals are wirelessly transmitted to a data receiver, which processes them; the processed signals are transmitted back to the cap, where the data can be stored, or used to trigger a response.

This brain computer interface has several potentially useful applications. If the user is driving and becomes sleepy, for example, the device can detect this and issue an audio warning. Eventually, researchers suggest, it may also allow the wearer to control home electronics such as TVs, computers, and air conditioners just by thinking about them. This technology could be particularly useful for the elderly and the physically disabled. (For more on this research: www.physorg.com/news130152277.html.)

The possibilities are tantalizing. Just imagine if they could install one of those things into a "Damn Seagulls" cap.

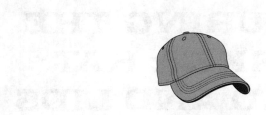

5

CAPTURING THE MARKET: HAT WORLD AND LIDS

How a couple of guys from the Midwest
parlayed a simple idea into a retail empire;
Lids and Hat World—two businesses that created
the infrastructure for America's cap culture.

IN the early 1990s, if you wanted to buy a ball cap displaying the logo of your favorite sports team, you often had to search. There weren't any stores that sold just baseball caps back then, and the sporting goods chains that carried ball caps usually kept a limited selection in stock.

A number of people took note of this; a few decided to change it. Among them were Ben Fischman, a student at Boston University, and Glenn Campbell and Scott Molander, sports store manager trainers from Indiana. In 1993, Fischman opened a ball cap kiosk at a mall in Massachusetts; he called it Lids. The next year, Campbell and Molander drew up a business plan for an Indiana cap store that they would call Hat World.

Within a few years, Hat World and Lids were national chains, with stores in hundreds of shopping malls across America. Both chains played important roles in the popularization of the baseball cap, anticipating the increase in demand for ball caps and the diversification of the industry. In 2001, Hat World acquired Lids. It took over several smaller chains in the ensuing years. Today, Hat World, Inc. is a division of Genesco and is by far the world's leading retailer of baseball caps, with more than 880 stores in the United States and Canada, operating under the names Lids, Hat World, Lids Kids, Hat Shack, Hat Zone, Head Quarters, and Cap Connection. The company's revenues for 2008 were about four hundred million dollars.

This is the story of Hat World and Lids.

PERFECT FIT

Ben Fischman was always a cap wearer. Go back to his earliest photos, he says, and you'll find a ball cap on his head. But in 1993, Fischman noticed something that both surprised and intrigued him: Everyone else, it seemed, was wearing ball caps, too.

He was a junior at Boston University at the time, working toward a degree in communications. "The idea really came to me sitting in the back of a lecture hall, in the college of communications at B.U., looking at all these white, blue, and black domes in front of me," he says. "Everybody was wearing a cap."

The ball cap was becoming important to young people, he sensed, "like their jeans." But the manufacturers and marketers of ball caps didn't seem to understand that, Fischman says. "I remember walking around a local mall with some friends. We went into four or five different stores and they had a lot of hats but not a single one that we wanted. And that's when I realized that the hat-makers had it all backwards: The hat-makers thought it was the decoration that mattered, what was on the cap. But it wasn't the decoration, it was how the hat fit. That's what mattered to people. And hence, the idea was born."

Fischman and his friend Doug Karp sensed an opportunity to make some money selling ball caps during the holiday season. They approached the Atrium Mall near Boston and rented kiosk space (Karp's father was CEO of the corporation that owned the mall, but, says Fischman, "We paid rent like everyone else."). Inside the mall was an old Model T Ford; Fischman proposed renting the car and using it to display their product ("It would be fun, peddling hats out of an old car.").

One of the most popular college caps at the time was made by a company called The Game. It featured a distinctive design—three horizontal bars across the crown front , with the school name between the top two bars. The design was clean and attractive; the fit was comfortable, unlike the stiffer, boxier caps found in sporting goods stores. It was also a particularly sought-after cap among college students. There was just one problem, Fischman says: You couldn't find it in retail stores.

When Fischman called The Game, he was told that the three-bar cap had been discontinued. "I said, 'Is there any way I can get any?' They said, 'Well, we've got a bunch of close-outs.' I said, 'We'll take them.'"

Fischman bought dozens of caps for $1.25 apiece, and priced them at about seventeen dollars each. The Model T Lids kiosk opened for business on the morning after Thanksgiving of 1993. "I remember waking up that morning and thinking, 'Wow, I'm really doing this,' and worrying that I'd bought too much inventory," he says. "But I remember at about one o'clock that day I'd sold out every cap from our first order. The excitement of that, the exhilaration of people coming from the local colleges who had heard about this cool hat store—it just rolled from there."

He called The Game supplier and asked for more caps. "I kept ordering and ordering. I was the only one in the country that wanted what they thought were these old close-outs. But to my customer, they were gold. And the reason they were gold was they had a very simple, clean design, and, mostly, because the hat was malleable. You could break it in to fit your head perfectly. From that time on, I strived to really create the great fitting hat."

Although Lids never actually manufactured caps, Fischman would work with suppliers to help develop styles, including garment-washed caps that, he says, "looked like they were almost painted on your head." The idea of a malleable cap with a clean design became a trademark of the Lids chain.

But in the winter of 1993, Lids was still a single kiosk in a single mall—and Fischman had to decide what to do with it. Clearly, there was a market for ball caps and room to grow. "The question then became, Do I want to do this? I'm a junior in college. I didn't really expect this."

In January 1994, he went to a venture capital firm in Boston and acquired the financial backing to open another five stores. Each one did better than the one before it, he says, and Fischman began to realize that Lids could become a national brand.

Sometimes, he recalls, people would walk into one of the stores and ask, "'Why didn't I think of this?' The simplicity of the idea was a big part of it, and the notion that we were experts at something that nobody ever thought needed expertise in the past. Some things are so simple that people don't think of doing them."

Fischman managed to graduate from B.U., although "75 percent of my attention was focused on Lids and 25 percent on school," he says. His working knowledge of the product and the customer, mixed with his passion for business, were keys to Lids' initial success. But Fischman was still in his early twenties and lacked the expertise to lead the company in the ways it was poised to grow—and he knew that. "To this day, I talk about the lesson that I learned through necessity in my first two years at Lids," he says. "I learned that for this to be as successful as I wanted it to be, I needed to surround myself with a team of people who knew a heck of a lot more than I did about how to build a retail company." The team included CEO Jack Chadsey, a former senior executive with such retail chains as Target, Kohl's, and May Department Stores.

For several years, Lids' growth was spectacular. The company expanded to 95 stores in 1996, 182 stores in 1997, 313 stores in 1998,

388 stores in 1999, and 413 stores in 2000. Fischman left the company in 2000 to work for a Boston-based venture firm. Now thirty-seven, he is the CEO of Retail Convergence Inc., which operates SmartBargains (www.smartbargains.com), a discount online shopping site, and RueLaLa, a high-end, invitation-only shopping community.

Lids' industry-leading growth eventually caught up with it. By the holiday season of 2000-2001, the chain had over-expanded and over-spent on its infrastructure. In 2001, Lids was forced to file Chapter 11 bankruptcy protection.

Lids remains a well-regarded brand name, both nationally and internationally. The majority of Hat World stores today use the name. "The Lids success was about a great group of people who took a sleepy item and made it an important part of the wardrobe," says Fischman, when asked about the influence of the company he started.

Fischman adds that he's still a customer. "I buy all my hats there."

SEEING WHAT WASN'T THERE

Glenn Campbell and Scott Molander are Midwesterners who met while working as manager trainers for the Foot Locker sporting goods chain in Indiana. Molander grew up on a farm in Crosby, North Dakota, a few miles from the Canadian border. He played basketball in high school and attended Dickinson State College on a hoops scholarship ("I was the smallest forward in the conference," he says), earning a degree in business administration.

Glenn Campbell was raised in Cape Girardeau, in Southeastern Missouri. His father was a candy and tobacco salesman and he began working in retail himself at age sixteen, at a small, locally owned grocery. "My parents couldn't afford much, so if I wanted anything I had to work for it," he recalls. Campbell was an avid sports fan, who followed the St. Louis Cardinals growing up and still does. He earned his bachelor's degree in marketing from Southeast Missouri State University.

Glenn Campbell, Scott Molander and Molander's brother Craig at the first Hat
World store in Indiana.

Both men took jobs with Foot Locker right out of college, Campbell in 1987, Molander the following year. As they got to know each other, they talked about someday starting a business together. In their jobs at Foot Locker, Campbell and Molander began to notice a customer who was invisible to most sports stores at the time. The customer would come into the store and ask for a ball cap that they didn't carry—it might be a Purdue or Indiana University cap; or it might be an NFL cap, for a team other than the Indianapolis Colts. "It was frustrating because we had maybe three hundred hats on the walls but they were for ten different teams," says Campbell. "Inevitably, people would come in and want something that wasn't there. 'Hey, you got a Packers hat?' Or, 'You have a Broncos hat?' Or, 'A Purdue hat?' And we'd always have to say, 'No.'"

As they began to see this customer more and more, they imagined a store that sold only ball caps. "Maybe there wasn't a market there yet," Campbell says, "but we thought if we give them a selection, we

LIDS/HAT WORLD AT A GLANCE

November 26, 1993: *The first Lids kiosk opens at the Atrium Mall in Chestnut Hill, Massachusetts. Lids exceeds expectations and sells about five thousand baseball caps during the holiday season.*

1994: *Lids expands to thirteen stores. Glenn Campbell and Scott Molander write up a business plan for Hat World.*

November 3, 1995: *The first Hat World store opens as a temporary holiday store at the Tippiecanoe Mall in Lafayette, Indiana.*

1999: *Lids grows to 388 stores and launches lids.com. Lids introduces Internet kiosks in some stores. Hat World grows to 110 stores and launches hatworld.com.*

2000: *Lids grows to 413 stores. Hat World grows to 157 stores.*

2001: *Lids files for Chapter 11. Hat World, Inc. purchases the assets of Lids Corp on April 13 and becomes the largest specialty headwear retailer. Lids corporate offices are consolidated to Indianapolis.*

2008: *Hat World, Inc. revenues are approximately four hundred million dollars. The company grows to 880 stores.*

could kind of create that market."

In their travels to shopping malls in the region, they noticed other things: mall shoppers tended to be impulse buyers, who would browse through stores and purchase inexpensive items if something struck their fancy. A typical impulse buy would be for twenty dollars—the price of a baseball cap. They also saw the increased specialization of shopping mall stores. Campbell gives the example of Bath & Body Works. "Women used to buy one kind of lotion, at the grocery store. Now they buy hundreds of different kinds, with different flavors. That market was created. We saw the opportunity to do something similar with caps."

Molander recalls bringing hats to Indiana from other Foot Lockers around the country and hanging them on the walls. "People wanted them. Everybody's from somewhere else. I'm from North Dakota and I ended up in Indianapolis."

By 1995, they had drawn up a business plan and were soliciting financing from friends, business associates, and Molander's former professor, George Berger. They figured they'd need about one hundred and fifty thousand dollars to open their store. Their idea was to carry a hat for every major league team and all of the local college teams, to keep a depth of inventory so that anyone who came in the store could find whatever cap he or she wanted.

One day, they went to a local bar and spent hours trying to come up with a name for their store. "Hat World was the best we could come up with," Campbell says. "Every hat in the world would be in our store. That was the thought behind it. The first signs had a likeness of me, designed by a couple of my good friends for one thousand dollars on a bar napkin."

Once they raised the money, they went to mall managers in the Indianapolis area, whom they knew from their work with Foot Locker. But the mall managers didn't see what Campbell and Molander saw; they thought the idea of a cap store was too narrow. "We thought once we had enough money, getting in the malls would be easy. But they pretty much shot us down," says Campbell.

Eventually, they were steered to the Tippiecanoe Mall in Lafayette, which was undergoing renovation and looking for temporary holiday-season tenants. The mall offered them a sixty-day lease.

Molander had left Foot Locker by this point and was working as a warehouse manager for Target. Campbell left his job, too, several months before launching the new venture. At first, he says, Hat World couldn't afford two salaries. "At Foot Locker, I was making about twice what I paid myself at Hat World. Maybe it didn't seem very smart. But I was thirty-years-old and to me you only get one chance to do this kind of thing. If it didn't work, you could go back to being the regular guy making $40,000-$50,000 a year, trying to support your family. That's how I went into it."

HAT DREAMS

Opening day for Hat World was November 3, 1995, a Friday. Campbell was alone in the store when it opened at 10 a.m. True to plan, they had acquired an inventory of about six thousand baseball caps representing all of the pro-sports teams along with a wide assortment of regional college team caps. All six thousand caps were on the walls—on one thousand shelves, which held six caps each. They retailed for $19.99 apiece

It took about an hour for the first cap to sell ("a pretty long hour," Campbell says). A woman came in and bought a Purdue University cap as a Christmas gift—a cap that the invisible customer couldn't find at Foot Locker. From that point on, business was strong. "Glenn called me that afternoon and I remember he said, 'We've got twelve hundred bucks.' And I thought, wow, we were really on our way," says Molander.

They had known that there was a market for caps, but didn't realize it would be so vigorous. At the end of their trial, Campbell and

Molander were offered a permanent space in the mall. They began to talk about additional stores. At first, their "dream" was fairly modest— to have five stores, two of which would be run by them, the others by family members or trusted friends. It took them about a year to open the five stores—in Lafayette and Muncie, Indiana; Champaign and Springfield, Illinois; and Indianapolis.

Campbell and Molander brought very different skills to the business, which Campbell believes is why they succeeded. "I'm a Type AAA, he is a Type B. He is the Ying to my Yang, which made for a perfect marriage. I knew the importance of hiring and retaining first-class people and treating them well. He understood the importance of good systems, good warehouse models. It never would have worked with just my skill set or just his."

Among the people Hat World hired was Jim Harris, their boss at Foot Locker, who became Hat World's CEO. With the opening of the fifth store, they brought in Ken Kocher as CFO. Kocher was a CPA, with experience as a corporate controller. He was also a sports fan, who sensed Hat World's potential: "There was no one in the space, really, except for Lids, and we didn't run into them much. It was a great concept that no one else was doing, with high profit margins. After two or three months, I invested pretty much my life's savings into it. Which maybe wasn't a whole lot—but it was a lot to me. I saw the numbers and said, 'You've got something cool here.'"

The company also hired employees that Campbell and Molander had worked with at Foot Locker, people who were "ready to go, to try something else," Campbell says. "The key to making our idea work was that we had so many good people. We had this hat dream, and once the dream got going, more and more good people came on board. We have so many good people now, we could put down hats and start selling socks and I believe we would be successful."

Hat World raised additional funding from Bluestem Capital Company in Sioux Falls, S.D., and took its first steps toward becoming a national chain, opening five stores in California, several more in the Midwest and in the mid-Atlantic region. Other people got the cap store idea around this time, too. But with the exception of Lids, no chain expanded faster than Hat World, which more than doubled its stores each year over a four-year period, growing from five to eighteen stores in 1997, to fifty-three stores in 1998 and to 110 stores in 1999.

CONSOLIDATION

By 2000, Hat World had 157 stores, compared to Lids' 413. But Lids had overextended itself and was starting to experience severe financial problems. "We had talks with them a few months before," Kocher, now Hat World's President, recalls, "to potentially combine our companies and it didn't work out. We had an idea that they were going to run out of cash soon, but we didn't realize how close they were. We thought they'd last a year and they lasted three months."

Lids filed for bankruptcy after the 2000–2001 holiday season. On April 13, Hat World purchased the company's assets for just $16.5 million—about the cost of the inventory. Before the acquisition could go forward, Hat World's management had to convince a creditors committee, representing the vendors who were owed money by Lids, to approve the purchase. It included representatives from the leading cap-makers—including New Era, Reebok, Nike, Top of the World—whose product both Lids and Hat World sold. "They wanted to be sure Hat World could take over and make it go, that we wouldn't become overextended and have problems, too," Campbell recalls. "They trusted us and believed in us and they all got their money back tenfold since the bankruptcy."

In one sense, the takeover salvaged the country's largest cap retailer; but it also recast Lids in Hat World's image. Hat World shut down 121 non-performing Lids stores, and made plans to close the company's offices in Massachusetts, consolidating the operations in

Indianapolis. Hat World transferred its business and merchandising philosophies to the remaining Lids stores, catering to a more fan-based customer than Lids, and providing a greater depth of inventory.

Business-wise, the difference between the two operations, according to Kocher, was, "They always had very deep pockets and we didn't. That's how they were able to keep expanding. I think money in a lot of businesses creates bad habits." Says Campbell, "We always operated as if we had only two nickels in our pockets."

By taking over Lids, Hat World grew from 157 stores in thirty-two states to 421 stores in forty-five states. Shortly afterward, Hat World hired a new CEO, Bob Dennis, a former partner in an international management consulting firm, with experience in mergers and acquisitions.

Buying Lids meant that Hat World suddenly had prime real estate in places it might never have otherwise gained entry. Some of the best malls in the country included a Lids store, and didn't have room for a second cap store. "It was kind of a dream come true," says Campbell. Suddenly, Hat World was the undisputed heavyweight champion of the ball cap retail store business. As David Gromley, founder of the Zepher GrafX cap, said in an interview at the time, "They're now the Microsoft of hat retailers."

The merger wasn't without a few difficulties. But Hat World again had the blessing of good timing: Ball caps were on the verge of another major cultural shift, with the explosive growth of hip-hop/youth culture and action sports.

During a three-year period in the early 2000s, Hat World grew from about four hundred stores to more than six hundred stores. It acquired the Hat Zone chain in 2002, Cap Factory in 2004, and Hat Shack in 2007. Revenues rocketed: In the year of the merger, the company made about $110 million. Seven years later, revenues had grown to about $400 million.

In 2004, the business that Glenn Campbell and Scott Molander started nine years earlier on a temporary lease in Lafayette, Indiana—after being turned down at malls in Indianapolis—sold to Nashville-based specialty retailer Genesco for about $177 million.

The sale was sweet, but also sort of bittersweet. As Campbell tells it, "For about three years, we were opening fifty to one hundred stores a year. Everything was going really well. And our investors looked at us and said, 'You know what? This might be a really good time to see if anyone out there would like to buy a hat company.' At that point, we almost didn't have a choice. Some of our investors had been in this for six or seven years and they needed to get paid.

"Fortunately and unfortunately, when you sell the business you no longer own it. Even though we were going to put a nice chunk of change in the bank, not everybody that worked for us was going to get that luxury. We wanted to make sure they had a job with a good company for the next twenty or forty years. The thing we wanted to make sure of was that our employees were getting a good deal. And I think they are."

Soon after the sale, Molander left Hat World for about two years. He returned on a part-time basis, heading the expansion into Canada, where the company recently opened its fiftieth store. He's now employed full-time again with Hat World. In 2007, Campbell moved back to the town he grew up in, although he continues to work for Hat World. "I'd been traveling one hundred and fifty nights a year for ten years," he says. "I've got four beautiful children. There are a lot of things that are important that I've kind of missed out on since I was thirty, and I decided I'm not going to miss out on them any more." Both men are vice presidents of the company.

Hat World's expansion continues, although at a slower pace than in the early 2000s. Kocher sees another hundred stores opening in Canada and maybe two hundred more in the United States. The company would like to grow into non-mall markets, such as casinos and book stores, and double or triple its presence in airports. Then there is the international market.

Hat World founders Glenn Campbell (left) and Scott Molander, in early 1996.

But predicting the future is a tricky business. "People wondered when we started if the cap might go out of style. They'll probably be asking that ten years from now," says Campbell. "What I say is sports has only gotten bigger. TV has made it bigger, the salaries have gotten bigger. I don't think there's any place else in the world that supports its sports teams the way we do. That's part of who we are. And for twenty dollars, no matter what's happening in the economy, you can pick up a cap and instantly you're a fan of that team.

"But who can say what's going to happen? Who would have ever thought you could open up nine hundred hat stores?"

The story of Hat World provides a compelling blueprint for success, although it's a tale that can't really be replicated. As with many success stories, Campbell and Molander came up with a simple but visionary idea at an opportune time, and were able to take creative detours around the obstacles that came in their way. The Hat World founders sometimes speak to business groups and colleges these days, but don't spend a lot of time looking back. "I always tell people I don't think I'm at the point yet in my life where I can sit back and say, 'Man, look what we did,'" says Campbell. "I don't think Scott and I take enough breaths to do that, although I think we understand it was kind of a once-in-a-lifetime thing. The dream was never to become this big. It was really just to have five stores. But once it got going and the train was rolling down the track, you either jump on the train and ride it or you get run over.... It's been a fun ride."

6

THE PROPER CARE AND FEEDING OF YOUR CAP

A complete guide to breaking in, cleaning, storing,
and caring for your baseball caps; plus, a very exclusive
interview with The Cap Whisperer.

OUR baseball caps can—and often do—become as comfortable as old friends. They make us feel good. They trigger reassuring memories, reminding us of where we were and what we were thinking when we first wore them. They provide familiar texture in a rapidly changing world. Many people hang on to ball caps that only an owner could love—grubby, misshapen, smelly—for reasons mysterious to everyone but them.

I know someone who wears a grimy old Florida Marlins cap when he goes out to the movies or sports bars and it invariably seems to change him into a younger man, who walks with the step of a teenager. I know a woman who laughs with greater ease when she's wearing her ball cap than when she's hatless; it's always the same cap, which she bought some twenty years ago, for about twelve dollars.

Increasingly, people seem reluctant to give up their ball caps, as if parting with them would be akin to parting with earlier versions of themselves. In researching this book, I was surprised to find so many people who still have virtually every cap they ever bought—dozens, hundreds, in a few cases (as we will see in the next chapter) thousands of caps.

But ball caps are fragile, and not really meant to last. A cap caught in a hailstorm, sat on by its owner, or used as a chew toy by the family pet may never be the same again. For this reason, there is a growing interest in the field of cap care. In recent years, dozens of blogs and websites have sprouted up offering advice—much of it contradictory—for cleaning, maintaining, storing, breaking-in, and prolonging the life of your baseball caps.

Of course, there are some folks who simply don't buy the concept of cap care. They think of baseball caps as inexpensive, disposable headwear—which, in a sense, they are. Those people might want to skip this chapter.

For the rest of you, though, who may have developed deep and highly personal bonds with your ball caps, this chapter will offer some recommendations for getting the most out of your cap—adding days to its life and maybe even life to its days. We experimented on a slew of caps (some of which did not survive), trying all of the popular ideas for cap care, and came up with our own suggestions. Here, then, is a guide to the proper care and feeding of your baseball cap.

STYLE AND SUBSTANCE

How your cap responds to treatment depends on its style and its substance—what it's made of and how it's designed. A wool cap, for instance, shouldn't be washed the same way as a cotton cap. A ball cap with a tall, reinforced crown will be more difficult to break in than an unstructured cap. First, let's look at the basic cap styles, then at the materials that make up most baseball caps.

STYLE
Pro-style reinforced caps
These six-panel caps include authentic Major League Baseball caps, and similar ones featuring a tall crown with rigid front panels. These caps feature a coarse, woven stabilizer in the front of the crown. They often look and feel stiff until they are broken in.

Low profile pro-style caps
These caps are the same as the pro-style caps except they have lower crowns and usually appear to fit more naturally on the head.

Semi-structured caps
A semi-rigid woven lining inside the two front panels of this cap gives the crown structure; but the stabilizer isn't as pronounced as in the pro-style cap. This cap can be either high or low profile.

Unstructured caps
These are caps without a stabilizer in the front of the crown. Sometimes, a removable crescent of cardboard will be placed inside the front panels as a temporary reinforcement. These are found in souvenir shops and retail stores and are the most common type of cap sold.

Adjustable caps
Caps with an opening in back, with either a flexible band, a Velcro strip, or plastic pegs, so that one size fits all. Most caps sold today are adjustable.

Fitted caps
These are made to fit individual head sizes and have a covered back. Major League Baseball players all wear fitted caps.

Mesh caps

These caps have a plastic mesh back and tall foam front panels. They usually are five- or six-paneled and feature a snap-lock plastic adjustable band in back. They are inexpensive and often sold in department stores and convenience stores.

SUBSTANCE

Most baseball caps are made of cotton twill, a closely woven cotton substance that is durable and easily washed. Some caps are blends of cotton and polyester. Professional baseball caps were made of wool until 2007 and are now polyester. The reinforcement in the front of baseball caps is usually a stiff weave of cotton fibers called buckram. The visor boards are generally made of a plastic blend, not cardboard. Most ball caps contain a tag inside the band indicating what materials were used; some include washing instructions.

Breaking in Your Cap

The two parts of the baseball cap most in need of breaking in are the crown and the bill. Caps with reinforced, tall crowns can be especially challenging. Usually, they don't look or fit quite right at first: the bill may seem too flat, the crown too stiff, and the logo panels boxy. There's no chemistry between the cap and your head. The cap looks like it wants to be somewhere else. Part of the appeal of the ball cap is its "casualness"; new caps sometimes seem anything but casual.

Unstructured caps, on the other hand, require minimal breaking in.

The most tried and true way of breaking in a baseball cap is simply to wear it and sweat in it, letting it grow accustomed to your head. But there are a few tricks that can speed up the process, lessening your cap's "awkward stage."

Breaking in the Crown

There are various ways of breaking in the front panels of a buckram-stabilized cap. Here are our suggestions:

- **For adjustable caps:** Open up the back of the cap to the largest size possible and then re-close. Clasp the bill of the cap between your thumb and forefinger and then bend it so that the right and left sides are touching. Next, tuck the bill underneath the cap and pull it through the open space in the back (above the adjustable strap). Keep the cap folded like this for several hours. This creates a natural-looking contour and broken-in look without damaging the cap. Repeat this exercise as necessary.

- **For non-adjustable caps:** Bend the sides of the bill together, as above, tuck the bill inside the cap, and hold it in place. This takes some of the stiffness out of the crown.

- **Soak your cap.** Molding a reinforced cap to your head can be effectively hastened by soaking the cap in warm water before wearing. Then, place the cap on your head and let it dry. The cap will mold to the shape of your head, and some of the boxy stiffness in the front crown panels will give. It's important that you wear the cap until it is completely dry, though, or it could lose some of its shape. Note: If the cap is light-colored, let it dry in the sun; if it is dark, try drying it both indoors and outdoors; depending on the material, the color might bleach if worn too long in the sun.

    A cap-store owner in Florida recommended a variation of this when asked about breaking in pro-style ball caps: Take a long warm shower wearing your ball cap, then continue wearing the cap until it dries. Voila: a fitted cap.

    A few caveats about soak-contouring your ball cap: If the cap is made of wool, soaking will cause the cap to shrink. Some cap-sellers advise purchasing a cap that is a size or half-size too large if the material is wool. (New Era, on its website, warns, "If you make the cap wet, it will take on shape as it dries! If you don't provide the shape, it will shrink to its own smaller shape.") If a cap shrinks too much, you can try stretching it by hooking the back of the cap on your knee, and pulling the brim toward you.

Polyester caps don't shrink, although some polyester blends do. Polyester caps may not contour to your head as readily as wool caps, but soak-contouring them is still a good breaking-in exercise.

Breaking in the Bill

Many caps come with bills that seem to have an unnaturally flat appearance. While the flat-bill look has become popular, some cap-wearers prefer a more "worn in," curved, natural look. Here are some ways of creating that look:

- Wrap the bill of your baseball cap around a baseball, a soda can, or a coffee cup. Cover the bill with a piece of cloth or hand towel and then loop several rubber bands around it to hold it in place (the cloth keeps the rubber bands from making indentations on the bill). Let it sit for half an hour. Repeat and adjust according to how you want the bill rounded and how it responds. Some people advocate doing this for several hours or overnight, but we found that if you let it sit too long, the bill can take on a permanent "too rounded" look. Visors respond differently to this exercise.
- An alternative to this bill-curving exercise is to pull the sides of the bill toward each other and then insert your cap in a coffee cup or drinking glass and let it hold that position for a half hour. Again, be careful not to over-curve your cap. This can also be done manually, if you want to hold the bill in a curved position while watching television, reading, having a conversation with your pet, etc.

- Finally, there is at least one product on the market for contouring the brims of baseball caps. It's called the Perfect Curve Bill Shaper, and it retails for about five dollars. We tested this product and found it to be a good deal for the price, although it doesn't seem to have any real advantage over using your own makeshift cap-curver, as described above. The Perfect Curve company also sells a number of other ball cap products at reasonable prices, including ball cap spray cleaner and deodorizer and a plastic cap rack for storing baseball caps.

Faux Aged
Some people prefer that their caps have a "lived in" look. This can be enhanced by washing your cap repeatedly in the washing machine (see the "Machine Washing" entry). There are several companies that sell caps with a pre-washed, faded look.

Surgery
The coarse, woven buckram material on the front logo panels of stabilized caps is what causes the crowns to stand up and, in some cases, make their wearers resemble train engineers. The purpose of breaking in the cap is to make it conform more closely to the wearer's head. Some cap-wearers have found that they can achieve this by cutting out the reinforcement inside the panel with scissors. This does give the cap a more natural appearance—when successful. However, after experimenting on several caps (which, sadly, are no longer with us), we recommend against it—mostly because it's difficult to pull off. First, there's a good chance of cutting through the front of the cap or causing other damage. And, if cut unevenly, the material can also irritate the front of your head. We recommend that, instead of buying a reinforced cap and performing surgery, you consider a cap that isn't reinforced or one that has a low crown.

Cleaning Your Baseball Cap

There are many effective ways of restoring a shine to your cap, including hand-washing, washing it in the dishwasher, or on the delicate cycle in your washing machine. Some dry-cleaners will clean baseball caps. How a cap is cleaned depends on its material. First, look on the inside of the cap to determine what it's made of and see if there are any washing instructions. If not, here are some suggestions:

- **Cleaning the Headband.** Wet a washcloth with warm water, and apply a light spritz of Spray 'N Wash or a similar product around the headband. Gently rub down the headband with the wash cloth, working out the sweat stains. Wash the band with clean water and let it dry.
- **Dirt, Lint, Dust.** Masking tape can be used to pull lint or animal hair from caps. Wrap the tape around your hand with the sticky side exposed and dab it on the cap. If there is a layer of dust or dirt covering the cap, spray with water and then rub a wash cloth gently over the surface of both the brim and the crown. Spray again lightly and evenly. Let dry in the sun.
- **Cleaning the Brim.** If there is a stain on the brim, hand wash with warm water and scrub at the stain with a wash cloth. If this doesn't work, try Woolite, Spray 'N Wash, or a similar product. After scrubbing, wash again with warm water. Hand-washing the brim is recommended for delicate caps.

Full Cleaning

Some people are reluctant to toss their favorite ball caps into the washing machine, thinking the caps will come out looking like unrecognizable lumps of wet cotton. They worry that the shape and the material of the cap will be damaged in the process of a full cycle. Their concerns are valid. We tried this with several caps and the results were not pretty.

However, there are several "cap-holder" products available, including the Ball Cap Buddy and Sport Cap Buddy, which hold the shape of the cap while it is cleaned, either in a washing machine or dishwasher. These devices, which are made of plastic and sell for less than ten dollars, can be found at Wal-Mart, online, and elsewhere.

Here are some specific recommendations:

- **Dishwasher.** This is an effective way of cleaning your cap, which we recommend. But do not use detergent, and do not let your cap dry in the dishwasher (this can distort its shape). Always place the cap in a plastic cap holder before washing. After letting the dishwasher run for one cycle, dry the cap on your head or on a form-fitting mold.
- **Machine Washing.** Cleaning your cap in a washing machine can give it a "like new" appearance but can be rougher on the cap than cleaning it in the dishwasher.

    First, place your cap in a plastic cap-holder. Wash on a delicate cycle, with just a sprinkle of powder detergent. If the cap has stains or especially dirty areas, try treating these first with a pre-wash spray or stain remover. Never dry your cap in a clothes dryer. Dry on your head, in the sun if possible. As a substitute, dry on a coffee can, although this can give the top of the cap a slightly unnatural look.
- **Hand Washing.** With more delicate caps, it is better to first try hand washing. Spray the baseball cap with a mild detergent and rub it with a wash cloth. Make sure to use detergents that are recommended for the cap's material. With wool caps, cool water is preferable to warm.

Packing your Ball Cap

The cap holder not only works for cleaning, but is also useful for storing your ball caps and packing your caps when traveling. This will prevent the cap from being crushed or bent in a suitcase. Alternately, you can tuck the bill inside the crown as described in "Breaking in the Crown"; this is more practical than packing the cap loose in a suitcase, although it may cause creases on the sides of the front panels. Another means of packing a cap is to stuff balled-up hand towels or a hard reinforcement inside the crown of the cap, then place it in a plastic bag with wads of crumpled newspaper or other materials as a surrounding cushion.

Storing Your Caps

When you keep your caps piled on top of one another or even sitting separately on a closet shelf, they eventually lose their shape. Ideally, caps should be stored on objects that mimic the contours of the head; this allows the crown and the bill to maintain their shape and form. There are several cap storage products on the market, such as the Cap Rack, from Perfect Curve, which we recommend. Hanging caps from nails or hooks is better than piling them on top of one another, but they still tend to lose shape and form over time if not worn on a regular basis.

Letting Your Caps Go

As with people and pets, all caps must go eventually, no matter how attached we become to them. Cap care can extend their lives, yes, but it can't make them live forever—or even as long as you live.

Unless, that is …

THE CAP WHISPERER

"The ball cap should breathe as we breathe. It should be an extension of us."
- John L. Powell

There are various legends about the Cap Whisperer, spanning many cultures and generations. One of the most persistent of these dates to nineteenth-century England. It concerns a rural hat merchant named John L. Powell who was, by several accounts, an extremely tall, eccentric loner with the odd habit of reciting passages from the King James Bible while gargling saltwater. Powell was an affable man, but his business sense was evidently so poor that when he decided to become a hat salesman, he opened his shop directly across the street from an already well-established and very successful hat company. Furthermore, because of an obscure zoning law, Powell was not allowed to post a sign on his storefront or to sell merchandise during daylight hours.

Unable to sell a single hat (even after trying an ambitious "everything-must-go, midnight-madness-sale"), Powell was forced to close the doors to his hat shop after just six weeks. By then, however, he had begun to earn a reputation as something other than a hat seller: He had a rare gift, it turned out, as a *restorer* of hats. Men and women would bring their worn-out headwear to John L. Powell's tiny shop after dark, and, within a day or two, their hats would seem new again.

After Powell's business shut down, people would ride out to his modest hillside bungalow and leave their hats on his stoop; several days later, they would return and the hats would be repaired—or, as one scribe of the day wrote, "Rejuvenated. By God, rejuvenated!"

At the time, of course, nearly everyone wore a hat. Businessmen wore bowlers; farmers and laborers wore straw hats and felt caps; society men wore top hats; women wore bonnets and tea hats.

Exactly how Powell was able to revive old hats remains something of a mystery—although there were several reports of the tall, stooped man hanging hats from tree branches in his back yard, talking with them, and offering them glasses of orange juice. A steady stream of customers reportedly made the pilgrimage to John L. Powell's home in the last decade of the nineteenth century, carrying their old and tired hats. (Among those rumored to have visited him were Sigmund Freud, Winston Churchill, Arthur Conan Doyle, Virginia Woolf,

Theodore Roosevelt, and Peter Pan.)

Many years later, Sir Winston Churchill would supposedly say, "He was a man who could gentle angry caps, old Powell. Meeting him was like opening your first bottle of brandy; knowing him was drinking it. He was the cap whisperer. That's what I knew him as."

Eventually, John L. Powell's work as a hat restorer brought him a decent wage, and he moved to a larger but more remote home in the English countryside. He hired a plump, comely blond assistant named Dee-Dee (a charwoman who had come to Powell weeks earlier with a damaged straw hat) to handle his finances and a burly bodyguard named Marion to keep journalists away.

What finally happened to John L. Powell is unknown, and his "cap whispering" techniques remain a secret. There were stories that he moved to America in the early 1900s (specifically, to Pierre, in the then-new state of South Dakota); that he had been hired by Churchill as a private "hat-man"; that he had died in a fluke cryogenics experiment (or, alternately, that he had died by drinking contaminated frog urine in India); that he had married a silk top hat and moved to the Samoan Island of Upolu, where Robert Louis Stevenson died; that he was hiding in Argentina.

All of these stories have since been proven false. What is known to be true, though, is that Powell fathered between eleven and sixteen children with Dee-Dee, at least one of whom, John L. Powell Jr., carried on his father's work. The tradition of "cap whispering" was passed down through two more generations and at some point carried "across the pond" to the United States. The current Cap Whisperer, John L. Powell, lives somewhere in the Western United States, and is still active, although, supposedly, he rarely takes on new clients.

This was all I knew when I decided to seek out the Cap Whisperer a year and a half ago. I had recently discovered two old ball caps in a closet at my house—caps that had once meant a great deal to me but were by then too damaged, I feared, to ever be worn again. Perhaps the

Cap Whisperer could bring new life to them. One was a skuzzy, old wool Washington Senators cap—sweat-stained, shaped like a flying saucer, and discolored, smelling of dead sheep. The other was a cap purchased on a recent trip to Switzerland, which, somehow, I had allowed to lie crushed for almost seven months beneath a huge box of books (during which time I had thought, with varying degrees of annoyance and anger, that someone had stolen the cap from my car). Unlike the Senators cap, this one hadn't been ruined by sweat or water or sunlight. But on the day I re-discovered it, the cap looked more like a .45 rpm record than it did a baseball cap. Both caps had sentimental appeal: The Senators cap was sort of a connection to my childhood—to long, summer days when a significant portion of my psychic energy was spent rooting for a team that was incapable of winning; the Swiss cap came from a family vacation, my father's last trip to Switzerland, it turned out. I had worn it while hiking with him in the mountains of Villars, the resort he had visited with my stepmother every summer for thirty years. A few months later, he passed away following a long illness.

After spending hours searching Internet sites for reliable information about the Cap Whisperer, I was able to determine only that he probably lived in Idaho or Colorado or Montana. He was very old but, apparently, still working. (I had assumed that the "Cap Whisperer" was named after the early nineteenth-century "Horse Whisperer," Daniel Sullivan, but several Internet sites claimed that it was the other way around. Some bloggers also speculate that this John L. Powell and the original John L. Powell were in fact one and the same.)

The only known photo of the Cap Whisperer is a blurry black-and-white image that seems to depict a very tall man in a dark coat with a long white beard and a white cap (although it may actually be a bare tree in a snowy field with icicles hanging from one branch). There is disagreement among bloggers over whether this photo was taken in 1889 or 1989.

Through various sources, I came to learn that, surprisingly, the

Cap Whisperer occasionally does consulting work, not only for the major ball cap manufacturers but also for Hertz Rent-a-Car. After months of trying to find a way of reaching him, I was given, by one of my cap sources (on "the extreme Q.T.") an e-mail address that, I was told, "will put you in direct contact with C.W.'s assistant."

I sent notes to this e-mail address but heard nothing in reply. For months. I kept trying, describing the conditions of my two caps in agonizingly detailed e-mails. Still, nothing.

I had more or less given up when, last spring, I received a call late one evening.

"He would like to see your caps," the faint-voiced female caller said.

"Excuse me?"

She repeated her statement.

"Oh," I replied.

"You must bring them to him, though."

"I will. Just give me the address. I'll be there."

It wasn't quite that simple, however. I cannot reveal details here about where the Cap Whisperer lives or how he works. That was part of the deal we struck before he agreed to see my caps. I couldn't even tell you exactly where he lives if I wanted to, because when I met his assistant at the airport—an elderly woman named, coincidentally, Dee-Dee—she insisted that I wear a blindfold during the several-hour drive to his home. I can only say that it is a beautiful and peaceful mountain retreat on a wide blue lake and that John L. Powell lives and works there year-round.

With his generous permission, though, I am able to reveal what the Cap Whisperer said about my two caps.

He spent the better part of a week in their company, while I stayed in a spartan ten-foot-by-ten-foot guest room, receiving three meals a day, of bread, water, a small portion of fruit, and several Cheetos.

After six days of waiting, staring contemplatively at the walls and ceiling of my room, I was summoned by Marion, the Cap Whisperer's elderly bodyguard. He wrapped a bandana over my eyes and drove me in a golf cart for what seemed to be several miles of rutted road. When he untied the blindfold, we were in front of what appeared to be a lakefront pagoda. In fact, it *was* a lakefront pagoda.

The Cap Whisperer was seated on the first floor behind a plain teakwood desk, stroking his abundant beard as I entered. I sat on the polished plank-wood floor across from him. Slowly, he reached under the desk and lifted out my Washington Senators cap. I took the cap and, in dismay, examined it. The cap was exactly as grungy as it had been a week earlier, although it seemed to smell worse.

After about seven minutes of silence, John L. Powell spoke, his voice barely audible: "This cap must be let go now. It is finished. It has no need, or desire, to breathe anymore. It wants you to let it go."

"But—"

"You are trying to prevent the natural order. You are holding onto an old, misplaced loyalty; you are confusing the nostalgia of a futile desire with lost hope. If you let that go, you will finally be able to empower this cap with the truth that you have denied it—and that you have denied yourself."

"But—"

"Sometimes, we do not want to give up on things because we think that giving up means failure. But giving up can also be the path to acceptance and liberation. Sometimes, giving up means casting off erroneous assumptions that you have carried with you as stubbornly as you have kept this poor old cap. In letting go, you can acknowledge the youthful energies that helped to shape you, but accept that those energies are not useful to you anymore."

"But that would mean—"

Before I could finish my sentence, he meticulously lifted a second cap from behind his desk—and I was rendered speechless. This cap, which had measured only about an eighth of an inch tall when I had handed it to him, was as perfectly shaped now as it had been on the day I bought it. I wondered for a moment if he had somehow purchased a new one and switched it out with my flattened .45 rpm model; but then I saw the initials that I had scrawled in the shiny band and knew otherwise.

"This cap held a special meaning for you, and you carelessly lost it. This cap knows of a sad time in your life when you struggled to understand how precious every day is. But then you began to lose that thought, just as you lost this cap beneath a forty-two pound box of books for seven months. It wants you to remember, and to go forward, living with the lessons you taught yourself in the days after you bought this cap. For that reason, it is new again, and it is yours to wear."

I cannot reveal much more about the Cap Whisperer, but he did allow me to say this: What the Cap Whisperer does is not magic. It is something that each of us can do, he insists, if we're so inclined. I spent a little time with him after he returned my two caps and watched him work on other people's caps. The physical process is not mysterious. He cleans caps in a clear mountain stream, employing various environmentally friendly spray-cleaning products. He uses molds to restore the shapes of the caps, along with a patented steam-dry process which I cannot describe. The mysterious part is how he communicates with the caps and how he determines which ones should be rejuvenated and which ones shouldn't. Most caps can be restored, he explained to me, as I was leaving his compound. But not all caps need to be.

7

CAP COLLECTING

How collecting caps has quietly become a new American pastime;
former Yankees star David Wells discusses what happened
when he tried to wear Babe Ruth's 1934 cap
in an MLB game; and, we visit with several cap collectors,
including the Guinness world record-holder.

"I've always believed that everyone should have a hobby."
– *World record cap collector Buckey Legried*

CAP collectors come in many varieties. There are those whose caps are keepsakes, mementos of places they've visited or events they've attended. Others collect by category: NASCAR caps, say, or Disney caps. Collectible markets have surged lately for skateboard caps and hip-hop caps, as well as for limited-edition lines from an assortment of fashion designers. Some people collect for sheer volume, covering walls and ceilings with their ball caps. Others collect for value, seeking out rarities, as a numismatist or philatelist might do (although value, as we will see, can mean different things).

Cap collectors may be young or old; male or female; Christian, Jewish, Muslim, Buddhist, atheist; natives of Earth or of any other planet. (Well, okay: There's no conclusive evidence that ball caps have ever been collected on other planets—although a team of prominent scientists and researchers recently called this "a mathematical near-certainty.")

What we *can* say is: There are more cap collectors on Earth right now than at any time in the planet's history. In this post-Cap Revolution era, ball caps have taken on a new, more front-and-center (and sideways) role in our society, while catering to increasingly specialized tastes and interests. And Americans—collectors by nature—have become more serious about keeping their caps.

Just as there are many varieties of collectors, there are many varieties of cap collections. The world's largest is owned by a Minnesota farmer, Buckey Legried, who has accumulated more than ninety thousand caps—more than four times as many as anyone else. But there are also hundreds of thousands of smaller collections, in bedrooms, basements, and living rooms throughout the country, reflecting the unique sensibilities of their owners.

COLLECTING HISTORY

"Every passion borders on the chaotic, but the collector's
passion borders on the chaos of memories."
– *Twentieth-century philosopher Walter Benjamin*

Sometimes, America defines its popular culture—and creates its cultural emblems—by virtue of what it collects. The desire for products with images of Elvis Presley or Marilyn Monroe or the Coca-Cola logo created a collectible market for each; and as the markets grew, those images changed from what they really represented—a singer, an actor, a soft drink—into symbols of the country. Collecting, in this sense, is a democratic, grassroots process of bestowing value on what our culture produces—whether it's TV shows, Pez dispensers, military supplies, bubblegum cards, lunch boxes, or Lionel trains. More than any other nation, America is obsessed with souvenirs of its very recent history. From eBay to *Antiques Roadshow*, we have made an industry out of recycling our still-warm past.

There are many theories about why we do this. Collect, that is. It may be related to some shared sense that America, more than other countries, is still inventing itself, still trying to mold its identity from the clay of the founding fathers' ideals and declarations. This could explain why so much of what we produce contains a blend of hubris and innocence. Or, perhaps it's something more deeply ingrained in our natures—a manifestation of our basic hunter-gatherer instincts; or the human urge to control what can't be controlled, to create order out of randomness; or simply a desire to link ourselves with the continuum of the past and the future.

One of the beneficiaries of our national penchant for collecting has been Major League Baseball. Even though football and NASCAR have surpassed baseball as America's favorite sports, the multi-billion-dollar sports memorabilia industry is dominated by baseball. The values placed on baseball relics have furthered the game's mystique and solidified its role as our national pastime. Baseball, our first sport, still holds reins on our imagination and our national identity.

THE CAP THAT RUTH WORE

On July 13, 2007, a sweat-stained New York Yankees baseball cap that Babe Ruth had worn in the 1920s sold at auction in New York for $328,000. Hunt Auctions, which sold the cap, called it one of only three known Babe Ruth Yankees caps. The auction price was reportedly more than twice what had ever been paid for a baseball cap. The sale represented an odd convergence—of baseball memorabilia, the legacy of Ruth, and the rise of the ball cap.

Traditionally, caps have not been a big-ticket item in the memorabilia trade. The serious bucks went for bats and balls and jerseys and, in a few cases, baseball cards (in 2007, the famous Honus Wagner T206 baseball card sold to a California collector for $2.7 million). But ball caps are showing an increase in value, say memorabilia dealers, and one reason may be the changing role of the cap in our culture.

The first baseball collectibles were player cards distributed in to-bacco, soap, sporting goods, and candy products, in the 1800s. But the self-generated collectible—the autograph—is what really built the mem-orabilia business. There aren't many signatures from baseball's earliest days. People weren't interested. That perception changed with the emer-gence of the country's first sports superstar, Babe Ruth, in the 1920s.

In an age in which the word "superstar" has been overused and de-valued, it's sometimes forgotten how extraordinary Ruth really was. Consider: The record fifty-four home runs he hit in 1920 were more than any other *team* total that season except the Phillies (who hit sixty-four); when he beat his own record in 1921, with fifty-nine home runs, the next best home-run hitter in the league had twenty-four; at his retirement in 1935, Ruth had hit more than twice as many home runs—714—as any-one else who had played the game. Ruth demonstrated achievements that would have been difficult to imagine without his example, achievements that changed the game, taking baseball from the "dead-ball" era to the big-league spectacle of a power sport. Ruth also changed the salary struc-ture of baseball, and the relationship between players and spectators.

The prices paid for baseball memorabilia have grown astonishing in the past several decades, and Ruth items are still among the most valuable. The bat that Ruth swung to hit the first home run in Yankee Stadium, on April 18, 1923, for example, sold for $1.3 million in De-cember of 2006, the most ever paid for a bat; in May of 2008, Ruth's 1914 rookie season baseball card sold for $517,000.

Until 2007, when Ruth's ball cap sold for $328,000, the most ever paid for a baseball cap was $151,000. That was for a Yankees cap once worn by Lou Gehrig. It was sold by Barry Halper in 1999.

Babe Ruth is still the top draw among memorabilia collectors.
In 2007, a Ruth Yankees cap sold for $328,000, more than double
the previous record for a ball cap.

THE HALPER COLLECTION

In the annals of baseball memorabilia, the largest and most significant private collection was that owned by Barry Halper. It's gone now, sold to various collectors throughout the country, although an integral part of it—representing about 20 percent—went to the National Baseball Hall of Fame, which displays much of it in the Barry Halper Gallery on the first floor.

Halper began collecting long before there was a real market for baseball memorabilia. In 1948, when Babe Ruth made his final appearance at Yankee Stadium, in a poignant tribute to retire his jersey number, an eight-year-old Halper was there. He approached the ailing Ruth (who would die about two months later) and asked him to sign a piece of paper. Ruth did. According to Halper's son Jason, "He was standing outside the stadium with a bunch of other kids getting player autographs and lucked out when Ruth happened to walk by."

In 1957, Halper had that same sheet of paper signed by Jimmie Foxx and Mel Ott, the second and third players, after Ruth, to hit 500 home runs; Ott died less than a year later, in a car crash. Eventually, Halper's paper contained the signatures of the first fifteen players in baseball's 500 Home Run Club. It sold for $57,500 in 1999.

Halper went on to assemble the most extensive and valuable private baseball memorabilia collection in the world, containing some eighty thousand items. When he passed away in 2005, the *New York Times* called Halper "a one-man Smithsonian." Yogi Berra referred to him as "The Babe Ruth of Collecting."

Halper played baseball himself, pitching for the University of Miami, but never at a professional level. After graduating from college, he went into his family's New Jersey-based paper supply business, Halper Brothers, which was founded by his grandfather. When the business closed in 1991, Halper devoted himself to collecting and to his family. In 1998, concerned about his health and estate taxes, Halper sold about 20 percent of his collection to Major League Baseball, which donated it to the National Baseball Hall of Fame. The next year, Sotheby's auctioned off most of the rest. The auction, held over seven days, brought in $21.8 million, the most ever for a single-owner sale of sports memorabilia. Every item sold, with 85 percent of the lots surpassing pre-auction estimates. Among the prizes were Lou Gehrig's last glove, which sold for $385,500, and a 1960 Mickey Mantle glove, purchased by Billy Crystal for $239,000. Other items included: Mantle's 1956 Triple Crown trophy (sold for $211,500 to Joseph Walsh, who displays it in his restaurant, The Stadium, in Garrison, N.Y.); Mantle's 1956 Yankees World Series ring (sold for $123,500 to Michael Fuchs, former head of HBO); the bat held by Ruth during his June 13, 1948 farewell at Yankee Stadium (sold for $107,000); a ticket to the first World Series, in 1903 (sold for $23,000); a letter signed by Rube Foster, the "father" of Negro League baseball (sold for $13,000); the first issue of *Playboy* magazine, from 1953, featuring Marilyn Monroe on the cover and centerfold, signed by Joe DiMaggio (sold for $40,250); and Ruth's 1933 contract (sold for $35,000).

The top-selling baseball cap in the Halper auction was worn by Lou Gehrig in the 1930s. It drew $151,000, the most ever paid for a baseball cap.

Halper was a legend in the world of baseball memorabilia. Other collectors and players made pilgrimages to his house—where, when they pressed his doorbell, they were greeted by the strains of "Take Me Out to the Ballgame"—to look at the collection and to trade stories. One of them was pitching star David Wells, who, among other things, shared Halper's love for the Yankees and for Babe Ruth.

A CONVERSATION WITH DAVID WELLS

For David Wells, Babe Ruth will always be baseball's gold standard. As a boy growing up in Southern California, Wells came to idolize Ruth. Not just for what he did on the field, but for his bigger-than-life personality off the field, for his impact on American sports and American culture.

"As a little kid, I kind of understood early on that there was something special about this guy, without really knowing the whole story of baseball and what he did. It just intrigued me that a guy could mean so much to so many people.

"There's no question the game would have been different without him. There wouldn't have been the home runs, the big stories. He saved baseball. He opened the eyes of a lot of people. I followed him ever since I was a kid."

Wells went on to become a great baseball player himself, pitching professionally in the Major Leagues from 1987 to 2007, winning 239 games. When he joined the Yankees in 1997, Wells asked to wear Ruth's No. 3, which had long since been retired. He settled for No. 33. On May 17, 1998, playing for the Yankees, Wells pitched a perfect game—one of only fifteen players in the history of Major League Baseball to have done so.

He was also, like Ruth, a player with an outsider personality, who liked to have a good time. "Everyone thought I was the party guy and all that, but you don't win 240 games being a party guy," he says.

Retired now, Wells lives in San Diego, where his home contains lots of Ruth memorabilia, including his jerseys, gloves, bats, and baseballs. Wells began collecting memorabilia in 1993, while he was pitching for the Detroit Tigers. "I bought a Babe Ruth baseball, single-signed, and then I bought a Ty Cobb, single-signed," he recalls. He decided to focus, as many memorabilia collectors do, on the Yankees, in particular going after Yankees baseballs from the 1920s and 1930s—the years of Ruth and the dynasty.

Perhaps his rarest item is the only baseball signed by Ruth and the

David Wells wearing Babe Ruth's 1934 cap at Yankee Stadium on June 28, 1997. The Yankee pitcher was forced to take it off after the first inning.

two men who surpassed him on the home run list—Hank Aaron and Barry Bonds. Wells asked Bonds to sign the ball himself. "I talked to Barry and he's never signed another Babe Ruth ball. So I think it's documented that I'm the only one who has this baseball."

Another rarity is a Babe Ruth cap from 1934. Wells bought it for $35,000 in May 1997, as the cap was about to be auctioned. At the time, it was the most paid for a ball cap.

About a month later, Wells wore the Ruth cap on the field, pitching in Yankee Stadium against the Cleveland Indians. It was an incident that is now nearly as famous as Wells' perfect game. Here's what he says about it:

BCN: Did you think, when you bought the Babe Ruth cap, that you would actually wear it in a game?
DW: Yeah. I told everybody that. I kept claiming that I was going to wear it and (Yankees coach) Joe Torre kept saying, "No you're not going to wear it." And I said, "My ass. I'm going to wear it." Joe was really against me wearing it in a game. I could never really understand why. As great a ballplayer as he was, and understanding the history as he does, I'm thinking, Why wouldn't you want a guy to wear it? I couldn't understand. But, you know, he's very traditional, obviously.

BCN: What were the circumstances that prompted you to wear it?
DW: I had told everybody I was going to do it. And he came up to me and said, "You're not going to wear that hat." I said, "I am going to wear that hat, Joe." And so, I was warming up in the bullpen for the game against Cleveland, you know. And it was kind of cool because when Babe Ruth made his last speech at Yankee Stadium and he was leaning on Bob Feller's bat (on June 13, 1948, when his number was retired), he was there at Yankee Stadium and the Yankees were playing the Cleveland Indians.

So I walked out from the bullpen into the dugout and (Torre) was kind of looking at me and looking at the hat that I was wearing when I went into the tunnel. The Ruth cap was in my locker. I pulled it out and just ran out onto the field before he could say anything.

BCN: And then, at a certain point, he realized. What was his reaction?
DW: He got pissed. When I came into the dugout after the first half of the first inning, he said, "Take it off!" He was all mad. He said, "It's not a required uniform." I mean, it had "NY" on it; it was just a little smaller. Guys wear hats all the time that are old and they're all sweaty and nasty. He just made a big deal out of something that should never have been such a big deal. It's history. He knew how much I admired Babe Ruth and all that. So, from that point on, I thought he was just a cheesy character.

BCN: What was your reaction when he asked you to take it off? Were you upset?
DW: Was I. I wanted to call him every name in the book. I don't know what his problem was. Maybe I wasn't one of his favorite pupils on the team. But looking back at it, I couldn't care less. I wanted to wear the hat and I did it and there was nothing he could do about it. He ended up fining me, which I also thought was pretty cheesy. I took the money into his office and threw it at him. He got twenty-five hundred bucks out of me. But it was worth paying twenty-five hundred dollars to do it. If he needed the money that bad, he should've just asked for it. I would have given it to him.

BCN: Why was it so important to you to wear Ruth's cap?
DW: Because of who he was, what he did for the game. As soon as I bought it, I thought it'd be kind of cool to wear it in a game and I was talking to people, and they said, "Yeah do it, man." They were egging me on a little bit. I thought it would kind of bring back history. And me being such a big Babe Ruth fan. And you know what? Everybody

loved it. I got letters—still to this day, people say that was just the coolest thing, you out there wearing Babe Ruth's cap.

BCN: It was pretty cool.

DW: You're damn straight it was.

BCN: Looking back on that day, is there anything you would have done differently?

DW: Not really. I just wish I could have worn it for the whole game because after I took it off, I got my butt kicked. I only got into the third inning. The first inning I wore it and I came out unscathed. And after it came off, it was the first time Cleveland beat me in like two years. I had a pretty good track record against Cleveland. (The Yankees, ahead 3–0 after the first inning, lost 12–8).

BCN: So did the cap incident actually play a role in the loss?

DW: I don't know. It's not like I said, "Oh, I'm not going to pitch well any more because I have to take the hat off." No, trust me. I don't care what cap I'm wearing. I'm going to go out there and give you 110 percent. I just ended up getting an ass-whipping. But it's weird, the only inning I had the cap on was the inning I did the best.

BCN: What's the story behind the cap itself?

DW: It's from 1934. The story was, (Ruth) came in and they promised him that he would be a player/manager because he wanted to manage. So he came in to the clubhouse and they told him, "No, you're not going to be a manager," and he got all pissed off and he threw his hat across the clubhouse. One of the clubhouse kids brought it back to him and said, "Here you go, Mr. Ruth," and he said, "No, you enjoy it." So the kid in the clubhouse passed it down to his kid and that's who I bought it from.

BCN: Is it true that it's one of only three known Babe Ruth Yankees caps?

DW: There are probably some out there that we don't hear about, in private collections that they don't share. Maybe they're scared of getting robbed. You never know until they come out and say publicly, "I have this." But three sounds like a good number to me.

BCN: Is the cap your most valuable item?

DW: I don't think of it so much in terms of monetary value. I have all my stuff insured and put away in a safe place but I don't really think (that way). To me, the value is determined by the history, the importance in the history—like if you have something from the 1927 Yankees, you know, that's pretty valuable. Or that cap, because it may have been the last one he ever wore as a Yankee.

BCN: You just mentioned the 1927 Yankees, which some people say was the greatest team ever. But others say the 1998 Yankees. You were part of that team and had a great season, going 18–4 and pitching the perfect game. Which was better—or can you be objective about it?

DW: I'd say the '98 Yankees were probably the best team. We won 114 games and won the World Series. I think that we had a better team. But they had a more powerful team. They had Murderer's Row and some really big hitters. We didn't have a lot of guys who hit a lot of home runs. But it was a team effort and everybody did their part to win all those games. You can argue it either way—that '27 was the best team ever or '98 was the best team ever. I would take '98 over '27. But it was just cooler back in '27. A lot cooler. It was Babe Ruth.

THE THIRD SIGNATURE

Don Gunther owns one of the most distinguished baseball memorabilia collections in the country. When he built his home in Southwest Florida six years ago, Gunther included a wing for his growing collection of bats, balls, caps, trophies, and other items. The memorabilia rooms resemble a small baseball shrine, with Gunther's collection tastefully displayed along the walls. Among his holdings are about seventy-five Hall of Fame baseball caps, each signed on the brim by the player who wore it.

"I started collecting caps about ten years ago," he says, "and decided it made sense to specialize in one hat: Hall of Fame caps. Whenever I'd see or hear about a Hall of Fame hat, I'd get on it."

Gunther is a lifelong baseball fan, who grew up cheering on the Cardinals, then became an Astros fan after moving to Houston. "I like baseball because I like history," he says. "It's more like America than other sports. It goes back, before the wars. It hasn't changed much. The stadiums have changed, but it's still pretty much the same game. I also like the statistical aspects of it. You don't have it to the same degree in other sports."

Ten years ago, Gunther retired as vice chairman of the Bechtel Corporation, the largest engineering firm in the United States. He'd worked at Bechtel for about thirty-five years, living and traveling around the world, running several divisions of the company. Bechtel builds airports and nuclear power plants. During his tenure, it constructed the Chunnel between England and France and the Hong Kong airport.

Gunther didn't get serious about memorabilia collecting until two years before his retirement. "What happened was I had a heart attack," he recalls. "After the heart attack, I was home for about three months. I couldn't work. At the time, I had a tiny collection of baseball stuff. But then I had some time and I thought, I'm going to see how hard it is to find some of these old balls. So I started looking."

Gunther has a collector's personality, he says. Previously, he had accumulated one of the world's best gold collections. During his three-month recovery in 1996, he merged his love of baseball with his instincts for collecting.

As he conducts a tour of his collection, pulling down Hall of Fame caps and telling stories about them, his enthusiasm is contagious. He

Memorabilia collector Don Gunther at his home in Southwest Florida, wearing a cap formerly worn by Nolan Ryan.

displays a Ted Williams cap. Then a Ralph Kiner. Bob Lemon ("That's a hard one to get"). Catfish Hunter. Luis Aparicio. Bob Gibson. Tom Seaver. Harmon Killebrew. Reggie Jackson. Nolan Ryan. Don Drysdale. On and on. There's one from 1951 signed by both Bobby Thompson, who hit "the shot heard round the world," and Ralph Branca, who pitched it.

"In order for a hat to mean anything, it has to be the hat that he actually wore with this team," he says. "So if a guy played on three teams, I may have his signature three times on three different hats."

Hall of Fame caps have probably doubled in value over the past decade, says Gunther. The value of a cap, he explains, is determined in part by how difficult it was to acquire the signature, not just by how great the player was. "There are different kinds of value," he says. "Reggie Jackson, for instance, signed thousands of things. But I never saw a Buck Leonard hat before. So that's a valuable cap because you can't find it." Leonard, a powerful first baseman with the Homestead Grays of the Negro League, was inducted into the Hall of Fame in 1972.

Gunther says the memorabilia business remains strong, despite a backlash brought on by the steroids scandals; but he's concerned that younger collectors don't have the same passion as his contemporaries. "They don't follow sports in quite the same way. When I was a Cardinal fan, I lived and died every pitch. It isn't quite as intense with young people anymore."

As impressive as Gunther's cap collection is, his real specialty is bats. He has about four hundred of them, including complete sets of Hall of Fame and World Series bats. There are other rarities here, including a Willie Mays 1986 Golden Glove, a bat signed by 111 Hall of Fame players (and five who aren't in the Hall of Fame, one of them Pete Rose), World Series and Super Bowl trophies, football helmets, boxing gloves.

Memorabilia collectors are, almost by definition, storytellers. How could they not be? Before his guest leaves, Gunther tells the story of what he calls his "favorite signature." He pulls out one of the rarer items in his collection—a 1961 bat signed by both Mickey Mantle and Roger Maris. "You don't see many of these," he says, displaying the bat in his open palms. "That's pretty unusual. I'd never seen it before. I heard about it. I was looking for it. Now, of course, when you have something like this, you're careful. You don't touch the signatures. You don't want another player to write on it, because the value immediately goes down. You don't want any marks on it. So I paid a lot for this bat, and brought it into my house. It was sitting on my desk. One of my granddaughters, Allison, was visiting. She didn't understand why people had signed all these bats, what that was all about. So I'm explaining it to her and she's listening, wide-eyed. A wonderful little girl, about five or six at the time. And then I went out for a little while, and when I came back, she said, 'I have a surprise for you.' And she showed me the bat. Well, she had signed it, along with Mantle and Maris." Gunther shows the third signature, toward the grip, below those of the two Yankee sluggers: "Allison."

SMITHSONIAN COLLECTION

What does the venerable Smithsonian Institution have to say about cap collecting, you may be wondering. A good question. According to Ellen Roney Hughes, curator for the National Museum of American History's Division of Music, Sports, and Entertainment History, "We have many, many baseball caps in the sports and entertainment sections." The museum began collecting sports equipment in the mid-1970s, noted Hughes, who has been with the museum about thirty years.

Ball caps in the Smithsonian collection include: a cap worn by Willie Stargell in the 1979 World Series; the caps Tom Selleck wore on *Magnum, P.I.* and Jamie Farr wore on *M*A*S*H*; a cap worn on September 11, 2001 by World Trade Center Fire Director Michael Hurley; a Vietnam-era green Army cap; a Defense Advanced Research Projects

An early souvenir cap from the 1939 World's Fair, now part of the
Smithsonian collection.

Agency cap with the slogan "Harnessing American Energy"; a cap
made of palmetto leaves and swamp grass in Palmetto, South Carolina,
in 1971; an undated cap from the East Ohio Gas Company; a cap
commemorating the 1939–1940 New York World's Fair; and others.

There are no baseball caps on display in the National Museum of
American History, however. But then, most of the museum's collection
is not shown. The NMAH has approximately three million objects in
its collections, and about 5 to 8 percent of the collection is on view at
any one time. "We haven't done an exhibition on caps. That's something that might be interesting to look at in the future," said Hughes.

The museum is currently compiling materials for an initiative it calls "Hip-Hop Won't Stop," which is expected to be an exhibition telling the story of hip-hop culture. The collection so far has several caps donated by the Zulu Nation and by Grandmaster Flash.

THE SPARK

Often, a lifetime of collecting is triggered by a single, unexpected moment. For Bobby Beaty, an auto dealer in eastern Tennessee, that moment came twenty-five years ago when a friend gave him a white ball cap from a company called Beaty's Seed & Feed in Cleveland, Tennessee.

"I put it on like I was going to wear it outside. But it was just so pretty, I came back in and I thought, I don't want to get it all messed up. So that's when I decided I would collect caps."

At first, he stored his caps in boxes. Pretty soon, he had boxes everywhere. "In the closet, under the bed. I was afraid Mrs. Beaty was about ready to run me off," he says, "so I built a warehouse and stored them there."

That was 1987. Beaty now has between 8,500 and 8,700 ball caps, all of them covered in plastic, never worn, lined up neatly on rows of shelves along the walls of his warehouse, which also stores his antique cars. Most are divided into categories: politics, automobile dealerships ("I have caps for every dealership in a hundred mile radius," he says), Coca-Cola, NASCAR (one has Dale Earnhardt's signature), novelty caps. There are some that defy categories: the Junior Samples cap from *Hee Haw*, for example, and an original FBI cap.

Most of the caps were given to him by customers. As long as a cap is new, it is eligible for his collection. He has had to expand the warehouse several times to accommodate all the caps, he says.

What compels him to continue collecting ball caps? "I don't know. It just goes back to that one that struck me as too pretty to wear. That was sort of the spark."

If there were divisions for cap collecting, Bobby Beaty would probably be the Southern Division champion. But it's unlikely that anyone, anywhere, will ever top the overall champion, a farmer from Frost, Minnesota, named Buckey Legried.

WORLD RECORD-HOLDER

Roger "Buckey" Legried is the king of baseball cap collectors. No one anywhere in the world has more caps than he does. No one even comes close. The last official tally put his collection at 82,792 caps. But it's well over ninety thousand now—and should top one hundred thousand within a year. He's in the *Guinness Book of World Records* as having "the largest collection of hats."

Legried lives in Frost, Minnesota, population 234, just north of the Iowa border. He has lived and worked there all his life, on a grain farm, raising corn, soybeans, and sweet corn. He also sells farm equipment. He began collecting ball caps around 1970, just as something to do. "It was easy back then," he says, "because caps weren't priced the way they are today. Many businesses were giving them away for free."

Most of the caps he collected were mesh-style "gimme caps," advertising agricultural products. "I started acquiring them like anyone else and just sort of put them in my closet," he recalls. "And then one day, I opened my closet and saw about a dozen or so caps on the shelf, all different colors and logos, and I thought, What am I going to do with these? And so I decided, I'll collect them. That's kind of how it got started."

Legried didn't set out to earn a spot in the *Guinness Book of World Records*. His only motive at first was to give himself an avocation, he says. "I've always believed that everyone should have a hobby. I don't care if it's collecting matchbooks or toothpicks or business cards. It's just good mind therapy. It keeps your mind occupied with something other than your work. And so that became my hobby."

Top: Buckey Legried, center, carrying some of the more than 3,000 boxes of ball caps to be counted by volunteers at the Corn Palace. Bottom: Legried talks to the media after shattering the world record. The final tally was 82,792 ball caps.

Early on, Legried set a goal of collecting a thousand caps. But that didn't take long. So he aimed for two thousand. Then five thousand. "When I got up to about ten thousand, which must've been 1976, the local newspapers and television station kind of became interested."

It got even easier, Legried recalls. As word of his collection spread, people would come by the farm and give him their caps, to help build the collection. "It went from ten thousand to twenty thousand to thirty thousand. And then after we got up around forty thousand, that was when I decided that I was going to pursue it a little bit harder and see if maybe we could get into the *Guinness Book of World Records*."

At the time, there wasn't yet a category for the largest cap collection. But an Alaska couple would soon create one.

Legried was meticulous about his collection, storing the caps in boxes—twenty-four to a box—that he special-ordered from a box company. He kept the boxes in a forty-eight-foot semi-trailer parked near his house. When it became full, he began loading boxes into a second semi-trailer.

For a long time, he put off actually counting out the caps. "Once, I was about ready to pursue it when a man down in Iowa called me up and said, 'I have twelve thousand caps for you.' And I said, 'Okay, we'll get them all boxed up.' Then, when we did that, someone else called up and said, 'Here, I have a collection of twenty-five hundred for you.' The numbers kept coming and I'd be thinking, 'Let's just get these in there first,' because then the number will be higher, higher, higher when we count them."

The decision to count the caps finally came in the spring of 2006. By then, the *Guinness Book of World Records* had an entry for the largest cap collection. John and Susie Cook, owners of the Tustumena Lodge in Kasilof, Alaska, had collected more than twenty-two thousand ball caps, which they displayed on the walls and ceiling of their fishing lodge. In 2002, they were recognized by Guinness for having the world's largest cap collection—then just over twenty thousand.

More than twenty-two thousand caps hang from the walls and ceiling of the Tustumena Lodge in Kasilof, Alaska. In 2002, this collection was proclaimed the world's largest, but the record was soon broken.

The Cooks were the first collectors in the category to be listed in the record book. In fact, they created the category, petitioning the Guinness company to include it.

But by the time Buckey Legried finally decided to count out his caps, he figured that he had about eighty-three thousand—well over three times the existing record.

In early April 2006, Legried's two semi-trailers worth of caps were hauled to the Corn Palace arena in Mitchell, South Dakota, about two hundred miles west of his farm. The Corn Palace—an unusual building with onion-shaped domes and Moorish minarets, which is decorated each September with giant murals made from South Dakota corn and grain—had volunteered to be the staging ground for the cap counting and certification. Legried brought some volunteers, the Corn Palace provided some. "They're an agricultural community, which fit with the agricultural theme on most of the caps," Legried says. "They just wanted to be involved."

More than three thousand boxes of caps were unloaded at the Corn Palace. Each box was opened and every cap counted. The final tally came to 82,792, almost exactly what Legried had estimated.

"That made it official," he says. "Then we put all the paperwork together and sent it to the *Guinness Book of World Records* in England. And in October, they sent us a letter saying that we were officially in the record book."

With Guinness certification, the collection is growing faster than ever. It has become more than just a personal collection, Legried says. "Now people give them to me so they can say that their caps are in the *Guinness Book of World Records*."

Legried expects to return to the Corn Palace soon for another official count. "We're just going to continue collecting and collecting," he says. "Someday, we'll have one hundred and fifty thousand and maybe we'll get to two hundred thousand.

"My goal is just to stay in first place in the *Guinness Book of World*

Records. Other than that, I'd like to see if we can get on Jay Leno or David Letterman or some national television show."

He has one other, somewhat more problematic, goal, he says: He'd eventually like to see the cap collection housed in a museum. "The problem is, it would take a wall ten feet tall and a half mile long."

Not all of Legried's caps are stored in semi-trailers. There are several hundred special caps that he keeps on the wall in his garage and in his basement. These include his John Deere collection, made up of John Deere caps from all fifty states. "Because of the fact that we live on a farm and use John Deere farm machinery, I decided many years ago, long before the Internet, to see if I could get a John Deere cap with the dealer's name, the town, and the state on it from all the fifty states." The collection now hangs in his basement.

"Once I got all fifty," he adds, "I said, 'I wonder how hard it would be to get John Deere caps from all the provinces in Canada.' So I have all the provinces in Canada now." These, too, are on display.

There are also the Branson caps, which a woman from the Twin Cities contributed after her husband died. They're white ball caps, autographed by all the performers whose shows the couple saw in Branson, Missouri, including Roy Clark, Willie Nelson, and Loretta Lynn. And the Rose Bowl collection—a thousand caps representing years of Rose Bowl match-ups that a man in Pasadena donated.

There are other stories: The Wisconsin cap collector, for instance, whose daughter called him one day and said he was going into a care center and didn't need his caps anymore. "All the caps were down in the basement. Some were hanging from the ceiling, some were on shelves," Legried recalls. "The interesting thing was, while we were taking these caps down, we found a half-pint of whisky behind one. And then on the other side of the room, behind another cap, another half-pint of whisky. And then another. He must've had certain caps that he kept whisky behind. I guess people weren't supposed to know that he was nipping."

Perhaps the oddest aspect of Buckey Legried's own story is that the owner of the world's largest cap collection doesn't wear a cap himself. "I never did. I'm just not big on wearing caps, although I'll sometimes wear a stocking cap in the wintertime." And he's not so keen on people wearing ball caps indoors. "That's a new thing. There are a lot of people who wear caps nowadays and I wonder if some of them are still wearing them when they go to bed at night. They don't even take them off when they go into a restaurant or a supper club. That kind of disturbs me a little. We had a young man in church one time who didn't take his cap off and I was up in the balcony looking down at him. I was just about ready to go and tell him, 'It would be nice if you would remove your cap in church.' But I guess the Good Lord must've heard me because at about that time he took it off.

"It's funny, I feel very uncomfortable with a cap on and the rest of the people nowadays seem to feel very uncomfortable if they *don't* have a cap on their heads."

8

CAP ETIQUETTE

The Do's, Don't's, and Don't Know's of cap-wearing;
advice from etiquette experts on what constitutes
acceptable cap behavior; and,
the Official Rules of Ball Cap Etiquette.

"It is a lot more complicated since the proliferation of the baseball cap."

– Judith Martin, "Miss Manners," in her column, responding to a question about when it is appropriate for a woman to wear a hat indoors.

IN the early 1990s, the principal of a Long Island, New York, middle school made news when he confiscated baseball caps worn by his students. Ball caps were becoming *de rigueur* among young people at the time, thanks in part to the example of music videos, and, increasingly, they were turning up in the hallways and classrooms of America's schools. This didn't sit well with Kenneth Handler, of Mineola Middle School. Handler's policy was to take away any cap he saw worn in school and keep it for a month. For a second offense, he would hang the cap behind his desk for the rest of the school year. "I'm trying to teach common courtesy and civil human behavior," he told the *New York Times* in 1994.

Several years later, the small town of Belgrade, Montana, became embroiled in a controversy after two boys wore their baseball caps to a Sunday church service. The boys' mother had approached the pastor before the service to explain that the boys played in a football game the night before and hadn't had a chance to wash their hair. The pastor, David Hansen, let them wear the caps, and no one complained. But the next Sunday, the boys wore the caps again—and they continued to do so each week after that. Some church-goers took offense, and complained to the pastor. Hansen sought advice from two veteran pastors outside the community and finally asked the boys to leave their caps at home. Writing about the incident later, he called it "the ball cap crisis."

In another case from the nineties, a Port Jervis, New York, high school student was suspended for five days for wearing a ball cap in class. In ruling to expunge the suspension from the boy's record, the New York Commissioner of Education stated, "At one extreme, one can hardly turn a page in a magazine that does not promote the wearing of hats, both in and out of doors as the height of youthful fashion. At the other, we hold onto the traditional notion that wearing hats indoors is a symbol of disrespect or bad manners. Moreover, I urge the community and board to consider the effect of such a policy in view of the needs of adolescents to assert their identities and independence, which are often expressed through clothing."

More recently, in 2004, a Scottsdale, Arizona, high school junior was arrested after he refused to straighten his ball cap—which he wore sideways during lunch in the school cafeteria. The school allows cap-wearing but not sideways cap-wearing.

Incidents such as these have occurred in numerous communities across the country over the past fifteen years, as the accepted rules about cap-wearing have been challenged and in some cases changed.

It isn't just young people who take their baseball caps into settings that would have seemed inappropriate fifteen years ago (and to some observers still do). Ball caps are worn with increasing frequency by men and women of all ages in restaurants these days, even in some chi-chi ones, as dining wear in general has taken a turn for the casual.

But there is still strong disagreement over the cap creep in our culture. Does personal expression really trump traditional manners? Do the old rules of courtesy and respect somehow not apply to wearers of baseball caps? If a diner or churchgoer is offended because someone in the room is wearing a ball cap, does the cap-wearer still have a "right" to do so? There are finer distinctions, as well. If you're dining at Le Bernardin, you don't wear a ball cap; no argument there. But how about at a Chili's? Or a Wendy's?

Are there any hard and fast rules about this sort of thing? Not really. In trying to come up with some, we took a backwards glance at the role of etiquette in American society, and elsewhere, and talked with several etiquette experts on the subject. Here, then, we share some of their thoughts and offer up our own official Rules of Ball Cap Etiquette.

A BRIEF HISTORY OF ETIQUETTE

"Manners are made up of trivialities of deportment which can be easily learned if one does not happen to know them; manner is personality—the outward manifestation of one's innate character and attitude toward life." – *Emily Post*

The custom of removing one's ball cap indoors, or when being introduced, has centuries-old roots. It may stem from medieval days, when a knight would lift the visor on his helmet to reveal his face and extend his hand to show that he wasn't holding a weapon. The removal or tipping of the hat is a conventional gesture of courtesy, often traced to ages-old military practices.

We can thank the French for the word etiquette, which first circulated, with its current meaning, in the court of Louis XIV. According to some accounts, a gardener at Versailles, upset that people were walking across his freshly seeded lawns, posted warning signs, or tickets, known as etiquettes, asking them to follow the designated paths, to "keep within the etiquettes." The term came to cover other rules of behavior in court circles and eventually in general society.

But the idea of etiquette goes back long before the French royal court of the late 1600s. The ancient Egyptian official Ptahhotep wrote out a set of maxims on papyrus, which still exists, instructing his son in the art of human relations. And Ancient Greek and Roman civilizations established elaborate rules of behavior.

In fact, by definition, etiquette has been around as long as civilizations have existed. From the earliest times that men and women interacted with one another, they devised conventions of behavior that enabled them to live and work together. While people and cultures have always clashed, and continue to do so, etiquette serves as a bridge among religious, social, political, and philosophical differences. It represents the better inclinations of human nature, the common, decent denominators of mankind. It also makes good business sense, particularly with the growing globalization of ideas and economies.

Rules of behavior were woven into the American fabric from the beginning—rules that were inclusive, practical, hopeful, and flexible, reflecting the ideals of a more perfect union, joining people of various faiths, beliefs, and ethnic backgrounds.

As a Virginia schoolboy, George Washington copied out one-hundred-and-ten rules of civility recorded by French Jesuits in the sixteenth century. Washington's simplified forms of these precepts (published as *Rules of Civility & Decent Behavior in Company and Conversation*) were the laws that he strove to live by, and that helped to shape his character. They included tips on how to dress, how to interact with colleagues, and, yes, how to yawn (examples: "In the presence of others, sing not to yourself with a humming voice, or drum with your fingers or feet; If you cough, sneeze, sigh, or yawn, do it not loud but privately, and speak not in your yawning, but put your handkerchief or hand before your face and turn aside; Labor to keep alive in your breast that little spark of celestial fire called conscience").

In the country's formative years, many of the etiquette rules Americans followed were imported from Europe. But as the nation began to forge its new role as a technological and economic leader, it developed its own ideas about manners. Men, in particular, rejected European-based niceties for a more direct approach. As author Nathaniel Parker Willis wrote in 1853, the inherent rudeness among American men was simply the result of "the peculiar uncertainty of men's fortunes and positions in this country, and the natural suspiciousness and caution which are the inevitable consequence ... Too much openness of manner and too free a use of the kind expressions of politeness would result in a man's too often being singled out for desperate applications by friends in need."

Willis, the highest-paid magazine writer of the time, urged a "distinctly American school of good manners, in which all useless etiquettes were thrown aside, but every politeness adopted or invented which could promote sensible and easy exchanges of good will and sensibility."

In the late 1800s, a new upper class arose in the United States, and with it a keen interest in how to best behave in "polite society." As Americans increasingly aspired to cultural sophistication, newspaper pages recorded the comings and goings of high society, and etiquette books instructed average Americans on how to act, during what was known as the "gilded age."

Here, for example, are a few pointers on table manners from the bestselling 1886 book *Rules of Etiquette and Home Culture, or What to Do and How to Do It*: "Do not talk when the mouth is full; Never indicate that you notice something unpleasant in the food; Eat soup with the side of the spoon, without noise; The fork is used to convey the food to the mouth, except when a spoon is necessary for liquids; A gentleman must help a lady whom he has escorted to the table, to all she wishes, but it is improper for him to offer to help other ladies who have escorts; It is very rude to pick your teeth at the table. If it becomes necessary to do so, hold your napkin over your mouth."

As the American Dream became fully realized in the twentieth century, and millions of people shared in the nation's newfound prosperity and prominence, a definitive etiquette guide was needed—a book that would teach our melting-pot population how to behave, during the American Century. Such a guide arrived in 1922, with Emily Post's *Etiquette—In Society, In Business, In Politics and At Home*. An immediate bestseller, the book served as the final word on taste and manners for several decades. It also made Post a household name and blazed the trail for Amy Vanderbilt, Letitia Baldrige, Judith Martin, and other etiquette experts. In 1946, Post founded the Emily Post Institute for the Study of Gracious Living, which continues to serve as a "civility barometer for American society," according to the institute's website.

By the time Post died in 1960, her book on etiquette had been revised dozens of times and was in its eighty-ninth printing. Ironically, her passing came at the advent of what would be a particularly tough time for etiquette in America. Each generation, of course, rebels to some extent against the preceding one. But the assault on manners and formality that began in the 1960s seemed particularly relentless—and prolonged. More than simply a natural cultural swing, it started as a long-simmering protest against American institutions and values. The lingering effects of this far-reaching protest include a general mistrust of rules and a casualness of attitude and dress. In the 1980s and 1990s, many workplaces loosened their dress codes. Before long, churchgoers were worshipping in shorts, sandals, and T-shirts. It was in this fertile environment that the Cap Revolution took seed.

Change in fashion often reflects some inner change in our national psyche, and perhaps Americans were just becoming more comfortable with themselves; or maybe they were expressing some deep yearning for honesty and simplicity. Whatever the reasons, American society has grown less formal and more tolerant in recent decades. Which isn't necessarily a bad thing. The acceptance of cap-wearing in restaurants,

for example, can be seen as symptomatic of a more general acceptance of customs, cultures, and ethnicities that are different from our own. But *should* it be seen that way? Aren't manners, after all, a reflection of who we are? Aren't they the outward manifestation of one's innate character and attitude toward life?

Hmmm.

Wonder what Emily Post would say ...

Emily Post, for decades the last word on taste and manners.

ASKING LIZZIE POST

Lizzie Post is the first member of the fourth generation of the Post family to write on etiquette. The great-great-granddaughter of Emily Post, she is author of the book *How Do You Work This Life Thing?*, a lifestyle guide for young people living on their own for the first time. She is also a spokesperson for the Emily Post Institute. Because her etiquette advice is geared toward eighteen to twenty-five-year-olds— a decidedly high cap-wearing demographic—we asked Lizzie Post for her thoughts on the rights and wrongs of wearing a baseball cap.

Author Lizzie Post, the great-great-granddaughter of Emily Post:
"There's nothing wrong with tradition."

BCN: Where do you draw the line with baseball caps?

LP: When you're hanging out with your friends, that's fine. In every college dorm room or college apartment I've ever been to, people leave them on. That's okay. It's fine if you're at a bar or a rock concert and you're with your friends. When you're with people your own age and you're in your own environment, that's fine. When you step outside of those parameters, you need to remove it.

BCN: Where specifically is it wrong to wear a baseball cap?

LP: Not at the dinner table. Not in church. Not at work, in an office job. Not during the National Anthem. And not when you're being introduced to someone. It's nice when you meet someone to show your face—both for your benefit, because they'll remember you better, but also as a sign of respect. It's symbolic. It says you aren't hiding anything. You aren't ashamed of being introduced. You are putting your best self forward.

BCN: How about at restaurants? Is it okay to wear a cap in a fast food restaurant, for instance?

LP: At any sit-down restaurant, I think it's a general courtesy toward the people you're seated with and those in the restaurant to remove your cap.

BCN: What about people who regard the cap as a means of personal expression? Are the rules changing at all?

LP: I think there's a bigger issue than someone wanting to express himself and that's respect. You need to respect your community and your environment. My generation grew up in a world where we maybe weren't always smacked for every bad thing that we did. The culture as a whole was a little more lenient than previous generations. There's less inclination now to say to someone, "Oh, you can't wear that here." It's a shame, because without knowing it, you often wind up insulting people and their traditions. It's important to look at it not as an issue of expression but as an issue of respect for the environment you're in.

BCN: Nevertheless, the culture has become more lenient, as you say. Does etiquette still matter so much?

LP: It matters, but I think it changes. Emily Post herself was very aware of the fact that etiquette changes with the times and that etiquette is actually something that's driven by youth because they're going to be the next generation. And so it's important to look to them. Yes, I think we've gotten a bit more lax, but etiquette is always going to be about consideration, respect, and honesty and that doesn't change.

BCN: If etiquette changes, couldn't the line between acceptable and unacceptable cap-wearing be changing?

LP: Sure. Rules do change, as people's attitudes change. It's possible that in five years, it will be more acceptable to wear a cap to church, for example. It's a gradual process. But I do think the baseball cap represents a more casual, everyday attitude, and there are places where that attitude just isn't appropriate. A few years ago, my family went to a really nice restaurant in Rome. My sister, my mother, and I were in cocktail dresses, my father was in a suit. The people at the table next to us were Americans, as well—wearing jeans, T-shirts, baseball caps. They were the only ones in the restaurant that looked like that. I was surprised they were let in. It was just wrong, and it made other people uncomfortable because it showed a lack of respect for tradition. There's nothing wrong with tradition.

'AGGRESSIVE DETACHMENT'

Patrick Allitt came to the United States from his native England in the 1970s to study American history. He has been here ever since. Allitt earned his M.A. and Ph.D. degrees at Berkeley. Today he is a professor of history at Emory University and the author of several books, including *Religion in America Since 1945: A History* and *The Conservatives: Ideas and Personalities Throughout American History*. Allitt calls himself an "Americanist."

In *I'm the Teacher, You're the Student*, Allitt cites his "intense love affair" with this country and describes his approach to history as comparative: "I look at the history of America through the eyes of someone shaped by British history and its legacy." He's passionate about teaching and tries to encourage his students to look at American history in new ways. In teaching immigration, for example, he reads off the surnames of his students, demonstrating the ethnic diversity and inclusive character of current-day middle-class America.

Allitt believes that when students wear baseball caps to class, they're projecting an attitude that is not conducive to learning—an air of what he calls "aggressive detachment." The classroom should be

Ball caps worn in a classroom can create an air of "aggressive detachment."

someplace special, set aside for learning and teaching, he believes, not "contaminated" by outside influences. He has, therefore, established a policy that ball caps cannot be worn in class. He also prohibits eating, drinking, and use of cell phones.

"The reason I make a point of forbidding hats in my courses," he told us, "is because hats were for many years a handy prop for students who wanted to sleep in class. Kids would sit in the back row, slumped down, hat brims over their eyes, so all I could see was a bit of chin. Eventually I decided I just wasn't going to put up with it.... Each new semester the demand is printed right there on the syllabus. I give students two copies of the syllabus on the first day of class, make them read through the rules, then sign and return one copy if they accept them.

"Emory prides itself on not discriminating against any group for any reason, and since I insist the boys must take off their caps, I apply the principle to the girls too. I'm relieved to be able to tell you that we've never had any fighting in class over the issue. I sometimes wonder what would happen if a student absolutely refused to remove the hat—we have no dress code and I would probably have to concede the point. Incidentally, I have no objection to yarmulkes and (among our few Muslim students) the hejab."

Allitt cites an incident several years ago when a student questioned his ball cap policy. He asked for her cap, then requested that she step to the front of the room and address the class. Allitt pulled her cap over his eyes and slumped down in her chair. The student blushed, refused, and put the hat away.

The professor's policy underscores a fundamental point about cap etiquette—or any kind of etiquette. When we move from one environment to another, the expectations and rules tend to change. In a classroom setting, where students have paid tuition to be taught, an attitude of "aggressive detachment" runs counter to their purpose in being there. It may also affect the balance in the classroom, not only for the teacher but also for the other students. In considering etiquette, it's probably a good idea to ask, What effect will this behavior have on my environment? The real issue is, as Lizzie Post says, "respect for the environment."

MARGO HOWARD ON BASEBALL CAP ETIQUETTE

Advice columnist and journalist Margo Howard is the only child of Ann Landers, one of the pre-eminent advice columnists of the twentieth century. Howard writes for Creators Syndicate and wowOwow.com. We asked her advice on the proper times and places for wearing baseball caps. Here's what she told us:

"I don't think students (should be) allowed to wear any hats in class.... In casual settings indoors, though, I don't think the old hats-off rule applies. The same would be true in restaurants. In a fast food joint, one could certainly leave the baseball cap on; in a fine dining establishment, no.

"Regarding first amendment rights to expression: I don't think you could make the same case for a baseball cap that you could make for, say, a yarmulke. While the wearer of a baseball cap may be a die-hard fan, that commitment does not approach the level of a recognized religion.

"And I do think there is a difference between a hat and a cap, as well as the purpose of each. I think baseball caps for young people (and even some grown men) are worn more to make a statement (I like sports/I am a fan of this particular team) rather than for warmth."

MAKING A STATEMENT

If it's true, as Margo Howard says, that the difference between a cap and a hat is that caps are often worn to make a statement, then we should be careful about the statements we are making when we wear a cap. The ball cap has, after all, become a symbol of America; how, where, and when we wear it determines what that symbol conveys. Inappropriate cap-wearing may even reinforce negative stereotypes of America—that we're crass and unsophisticated, that we don't follow rules. There's a difference between wearing a ball cap and wearing one inappropriately. Understanding this should be every cap-owner's responsibility.

THE RULES OF BALL CAP ETIQUETTE

Baseball caps should never be worn at:

- Church
- Work (unless the cap is part of a uniform or unless it is an outdoor work environment and the ball cap is accepted)
- Funerals
- Weddings (unless the wedding is outdoors and the bride is in flip flops)
- Government meetings
- The breakfast, lunch, or dinner table
- Fine restaurants
- Indoor concerts or lectures

No caps, please.

The baseball cap should be removed when the National Anthem is played at a sporting event; when you are being formally introduced to another person; during dedications or other ceremonies; and as a show of respect for the person with whom you are talking.

Generally, a cap should not be worn indoors at home.

Wearing a cap is acceptable:

- In stores
- At fast food or casual restaurants or sports bars
- On airplanes and in airports
- In libraries
- At diner or café counters
- In elevators
- On the golf course
- At outdoor rallies or concerts
- And in various casual settings

Even though wearing a cap on an airplane is acceptable, most people remove their caps during flights. Keeping your cap on, therefore, might be construed by some of those who have taken theirs off as inappropriate. The same holds true in a library. In general, removing your cap while in the company of other people is not a bad idea. It conveys a message of respect for those around you. This is particularly the case in unfamiliar situations and locales, where customs of dress and behavior may be different from yours.

Removing one's cap as a sign of respect is never inappropriate. If in doubt, remove your cap.

9

CAPS GONE GLOBAL

How and why the Cap Revolution has become an international
movement; ball cap news from around the world;
a selection of Old Cap Tales;
and, an international ball cap test.

"There's this notion, often expressed in my country, that America has no culture,
that it's all garbage. But the fact that everyone in the world, no matter
where you go, wears a baseball cap, has to be reckoned with."
- *Dame Glenda Jackson, quoted in the* San Francisco Chronicle, 2003

WHAT was reared modestly on the ball fields of America's national pastime has leaped over cultural, political, and geographic boundaries, and made itself at home in far-flung locales across the globe. There are few places today that ball caps haven't infiltrated. You will find them at coffee shops in Tehran, carrom parlors in Nepal, dance clubs in Ghana, dive shops in Fiji, farmers markets in Peru.

The baseball cap is embraced by many as a sign of modernity, as a gentle rebellion against tired traditions. In Myanmar, teenagers leave their longyis at home, pull on blue jeans and baseball caps, and go out dancing to techno music. In the Afghan capital of Kabul, caps, jeans, and denim jackets are seen everywhere on the streets, a look that wouldn't have been permitted before the fall of the Taliban in 2001. In the former Soviet satellite of Mongolia, a stuffy government-run bank hands out green-and-white baseball caps with the bank's logo, as part of a rebranding effort.

The ball cap has been recruited, too, as a political tool. When Libyan leader Muammar al-Gadaffi inaugurated the massive Gaddafi National Mosque in the largely Christian nation of Uganda in 2008—an event attended by numerous heads of state and religious leaders—organizers gave Arab journalists baseball caps bearing Gadaffi's image. In the West African nation of Burkina Faso, one of the world's poorest countries, President Blaise Compaore won re-election by a landslide in 2005 amid complaints of lavish campaign spending, which included distributing thousands of T-shirts and baseball caps emblazoned with his likeness. In the Middle East, a green baseball cap has become the symbol of the radical Islamic group Hamas. In 2005, Hamas reportedly ordered tens of thousands of green ball caps from a Chinese cap company, and handed them out to participants in Hamas camps in the Gaza Strip. When Hamas won its surprising election to the Palestinian parliament in January 2006, thousands joined in a victory march wearing the green baseball caps. In the midst of the Eritrean-Ethiopian war in 2000, journalists were taken to the front lines by an Ethiopian government spokesman wearing a baseball cap with the slogan "Our Victory Is Certain."

At political rallies around the world, ball caps are worn to show party affiliation or candidate preference. For better or for worse, the once largely non-partisan baseball cap has, alas, gone political.

CAPLOMACY

In 2006, Chinese President Hu Jintao paid his first state visit to the United States, a symbolic mission designed to help shore up relations between the two countries. Hu, who met with Bill Gates and President George Bush, among others, during the trip, spoke of the "extensive common interests" shared by China and the United States. On a tour of Boeing's plant in Everett, Washington, Hu wore a Boeing baseball cap, showing his country's solidarity with the aerospace/defense corporation, which has robust ties to China.

The year before, in a different sort of cap diplomacy (or "caplomacy"), the Dalai Lama wore a Washington Nationals baseball cap during a stop at a charter school in Washington, D.C. The cap had been give to him by D.C. councilman Jim Graham.

In 2008, Major League Baseball and the State Department's Bureau of Educational and Cultural Affairs teamed up for a mission to Panama and Nicaragua promoting baseball and American culture. As part of its mission, the American contingent distributed baseball caps in Panama bearing the American Embassy's "Estamos Unidos!" ("We Are United!) logo.

Although it's a term not yet found in most dictionaries, "caplomacy" is a form of diplomacy that will likely see its star rise in the coming years, as world leaders take full advantage of the ball cap's potential to transcend political and cultural differences and be an agent of change.

IN THE NEWS

"Look at the results ... From Croatia to Chile to China, every young person, even down to 18 months old, wears their baseball cap backwards and listens to rap."
– *Music producer/composer Quincy Jones, during a speech at Beijing University, Beijing, China, May 26, 2006*

The globalization of the baseball cap has resulted in some interesting and occasionally bizarre news reports. Here are a few that we culled from around the world:

Where the Super Bowl Means Nothing

One of the culture shocks that some Americans encounter when they visit a foreign country is that people in, say, Belgium, or India or Morocco don't care a whit about the New York Yankees or the Pittsburgh Steelers or who's going to make the Final Four.

An American visiting Chad in the spring of 2009, however, would probably have been surprised to see children wearing caps and shirts trumpeting the Super Bowl XLIII Champion Arizona Cardinals—particularly since the Cardinals actually lost the Super Bowl that year, to the Pittsburgh Steelers.

What gives?

Each year, the NFL makes apparel for the winning and losing Super Bowl teams, which it distributes immediately after the game. Because no one can predict the outcome ahead of time (well, okay, *almost* no one), apparel is made for both teams, proclaiming each the Super Bowl champ. The winning team's apparel is sold and given away immediately after the game. The losing team's apparel is shipped to the World Vision relief organization, which distributes it to developing nations, mostly in Africa.

The NFL-World Vision partnership results in millions of dollars of incorrectly titled, licensed apparel going to needy families each year. In 2009, Arizona Cardinals clothing was distributed in Zambia, Chad, Chile, Bolivia, the Congo, El Salvador, Romania, and Zimbabwe.

World Vision also gives away counterfeit apparel that was seized by United States Customs agents as well as other NFL, non-Super Bowl caps and other apparel. The combined value of sporting apparel given away in 2007 was about $2.5 million, according to World Vision.

The caps often go to regions of the Third World without electricity or running water, to children who have never before worn new clothing. As a spokeswoman for World Vision said, "They don't know who won the Super Bowl. They don't even know what football is."

A boy in Sake, Congo, shows off his Tampa Bay Buccaneers cap, distributed by the World Vision relief organization to children affected by conflict.

Ball Cap Identifies Murder Suspect

When Anna Lindh, Sweden's Minister of Foreign Affairs, was stabbed in Stockholm on September 10, 2003, her attacker left behind his baseball cap. Lindh died the following day; her killer remained at large for two weeks. On September 24, police arrested Mijailo Mijailovic on a probable cause charge. A DNA profile of Mijailovic matched that of hairs in the baseball cap, implicating him in the killing.

Banned in England

In 2005, one of England's largest shopping malls, the Bluewater Shopping Centre in Kent, banned baseball caps and "hoodies," which the mall claimed were intimidating shoppers. Several individual stores in England also banned cap-wearing around this time.

According to a report in London's *The Independent* newspaper, the Bluewater Shopping Centre banned ball caps and hoodies (better known in America as "hoods") because they "obscure the identity" of the wearer and promote "loutish" behavior, a mall spokesperson said. "We're very concerned that some of our guests don't feel safe in what is really a family environment," Bluewater property manager Helen Smith was quoted as saying. The ban was supported by then-British Prime Minister Tony Blair.

A children's charity, The Children's Society, though, called the ban "blatant discrimination based on stereotypes and prejudices" and said it infringed on the rights of young people.

We contacted Bluewater and were told that the ban is still officially in effect (the mall's Code of Conduct includes a prohibition on "The wearing of any item of clothing which restricts the view of one's head/face with the exception of religious headwear."). However, spokeswoman Debbie Greagsby said that the average shopper wearing a baseball cap would not be asked to remove it. The policy is aimed at people who visited the mall "with an intention of obscuring their faces," she said.

In a related story, the venerable Burberry company discontinued its line of checked baseball caps in 2005 after the cap came into vogue among young people known, in slang parlance, as yobs (which Wikipedia defines as "an uncouth or thuggish blue-collar person"). The cap was apparently also worn by some scallies, neds, and townies. The Burberry caps had earlier been banned in several British pubs because of their association with unruly behavior.

Cap Dispute Leads to Murder Charge

A Cape Town, South African man was shot dead in November 2007 after an argument over a baseball cap. According to court reports, two men arrived at the home of the victim, Godfrey Hendricks, and demanded that he give them back a baseball cap that one of the men said belonged to his sister. A witness testified that Hendricks refused, challenging the men to take it from him. The men then reportedly went to their car and returned with a gun. One of the men shot Hendricks and they fled, leaving the baseball cap.

Bulletproof Baseball Caps

Meanwhile, in the suburbs of Thailand's capital city of Bangkok, defense contractor Precipart has reportedly developed a bulletproof baseball cap. According to news accounts, the protective cap is among the latest inventions of retired Major Songphon Eiamboonyarith, who runs the firm. Songphon, who says he was inspired as a boy by the gadgetry on the American television show *Mission Impossible*, is sometimes referred to as Thailand's "Q," a comparison with the James Bond gadget-maker responsible for such devices as the Aston Martin ejector seat, the buzz-saw Rolex, and the bullet-firing cigarette. The bulletproof ball cap was designed with Thailand's police force in mind.

In Paris: Ball Caps Versus Skullcaps

Three days after a November 2003 arson attack at a Jewish school outside of Paris, France's chief rabbi Joseph Sitruk urged Jewish men to consider wearing baseball caps instead of their yarmulkes. "I ask them to replace the yarmulke with the baseball cap," he told Radio Shalom, a Jewish community radio station. "I say that to protect our young people." Sitruk's office said that as long as they kept their heads covered by wearing any kind of hat, Jewish men were following tradition. "I do not want young people traveling alone on trains or the Metro to become easy targets for attackers."

In February 2008, the JTA news service reported that many men in Paris had taken his advice and were wearing plain black baseball caps instead of yarmulkes. The news service called this "a noticeable change in the Paris fashion landscape, where caps usually are multi-colored and reserved for casual wear."

Kidnap Cap

In October 2005, masked Palestinian gunmen in Gaza kidnapped American reporter Dion Nissenbaum and British photographer Adam Pletts, holding them for about six hours. The journalists were not hurt and were treated well by their captors, who served them tea, dates, and a rice-and-meat dinner. The gunmen, who did not tell Nissenbaum and Pletts why they had been kidnapped, gave them baseball caps before surrendering the journalists to Palestinian Authority officials. Nissenbaum later said that he knew things would turn out okay when his captors gave him a souvenir ball cap.

"The group was called the Black Panthers (no relation to the 1960s radicals)," Nissenbaum told us, "and they were essentially a local off-shoot of Fatah militants. To be frank, they were keystone cops." The caps they were given were black, with the group's name stitched on them in Arabic.

The cap given to kidnapped journalist Dion Nissenbaum by Palestinian gunmen.

Buddhist Leader Fled Wearing Cap Disguise

In December 1999, fourteen-year-old Ugyen Trinley Dorje, thought to be the seventeenth in a line of reincarnated Tibetan lamas, fled his monastery in Tibet for India, disguised in jeans, a down jacket, and a baseball cap. Known as Gyalwang Karmapa or the Karmapa, he is the third-highest lama in Tibetan Buddhism, believed to possess the wisdom of his sixteen predecessors. Ugyen Trinley was just seven when the Dalai Lama, Tibet's spiritual leader, recognized him as the seventeenth Karmapa in 1992. Senior lamas had used omens, prediction documents, and a message from the sixteenth Karmapa to determine that Ugyen Trinley was his reincarnation.

Ugyen Trinley was the first Buddhist reincarnation recognized by both the Dalai Lama and also by Beijing. The Karmapa was enthroned at Tsurphu Monastery near Lhasa, Tibet, in 1992, in a ceremony attended by twenty thousand people. He stayed for seven years, but found that Chinese restrictions were keeping him from receiving the proper teachings of his lineage. In the winter of 1999–2000, he escaped into exile, traveling by foot, horseback, train, rickshaw, car, and helicopter, arriving in Dharamsali, India, the seat of the Dalai Lama's government-in-exile, on January 5. (Note: Although the Dalai Lama and many others recognize Ugyen Trinley as the Karmapa, some important lamas recognize another man, Thaye Dorje.)

Mme Tout-le-Monde

Photographs of French presidential candidate Segolene Royal wearing a bikini and baseball cap, relaxing on the beach, stirred a whirl of public interest and media attention when they were published in the late summer of 2006, several months before the election. The photos, which ran in two celebrity magazines, were apparently shot candidly on a public beach in the south of France. Some observers considered the publications a breach of the candidate's privacy. *The Times of London*, however, called the images of the fifty-three-year-old Royal "flattering" and noted that she was "unlikely to suffer" from their appearance. The editor of one of the magazines defended the publication, saying, "We chose to publish this photograph because in this photo she represents 'Madame Tout-le-Monde,'" or "Mrs. Everywoman."

Royal's cap bore the name "La Rochelle," a seaside town in the Poitou-Charentes region of Western France, where Royal lives and is regional president. Royal lost a close election the next spring to Nicolas Sarkozy.

Baseball Cap Capital

In Brazil, the city of Apucarana is known as "The National Baseball Cap Capital." Apucarana manufactures about four million ball caps per month, in approximately two hundred cap factories. This amounts to about half of the country's total cap production, according to Santiago Gallo, coordinator for international matters in the State Secretariat for Industry, Trade, and Mercosur Affairs.

The caps are sold to the United States, Mexico, Argentina, and elsewhere. Gallo sees the region growing as an export hub for baseball caps and expects to see a new cap market develop in the Middle East. "The Arab countries are very hot and the sun is strong, which could help the consumption of baseball caps," he told a Brazilian news service.

Red Cap, The Musical

The Australian stage musical *Red Cap*, which premiered in July 2007 in Mt. Isa, Queensland, was based on the 1964–65 miner's strike there and the charismatic strike leader Pat Mackie. The thirty-two-week dispute began with a demand for higher wages but escalated into a bitter conflict against the government that galvanized the community in favor of the miners. The title of the show refers to the Boston Red Sox baseball cap that Mackie wore during the dispute.

The Hague Cap

When William Hague became the leader of Britain's Conservative Party in 1997, he was expected to create a more modern image for the party. In an apparent attempt to do so, Hague visited an amusement park on August 7 of that year and was photographed with staff members riding a water flume. All of them wore baseball caps with one word emblazoned across the front of the crown: HAGUE. The British press roundly ribbed Hague for the incident (Simon Heffer, in his *Daily Mail* column, said Hague looked like "a child-molester on a day release scheme"), and the flume photo became an enduring image of Hague's first months as Conservative leader. He resigned the position in 2001. Hague is today Shadow Foreign Secretary, and continues to serve as a Conservative member of Parliament. He is also a popular author and media personality.

OLD CAP TALES

As the ball cap has assumed iconic stature, it's not surprising that a few myths have cropped up about its origins and influences. There is, for instance, the story that Albert Einstein invented the first propeller beanie cap at the same time he was working out his theory of relativity. Or the one that Julius Caesar wore an early version of the baseball cap, with the letters "IC" stitched on the front (the Romans, as we know, did not use the letters J, U, or W). And the story that Truman Capote once claimed that the cap was named for him.

These are what might be called Old Cap Tales, a variant of the urban legend. Although most of these stories have no basis in fact, that hasn't stopped people from repeating them (any more than we will ever stop hearing that Mama Cass choked to death on a ham sandwich).

In truth, the etymology of the word "cap" can be traced to the Old English "caeppe," meaning "hood, head-covering," from about 1225, which in turn comes from the late Latin "cappa."

These are a few of the Old Cap Tales that we have examined:

In some rural areas of France (and in a few select neighborhoods of Pittsburgh), the story is told that nineteenth-century Bible illustrations by French artist Gustave Dore show Moses wearing what appears to be a Pittsburgh Pirates ball cap. This is a fanciful interpretation of Dore's Exodus illustrations. (It is far more likely that Moses was wearing a Yankees cap.)

Norway's National Cap Day. Every April 11, many of Norway's 4.6 million people wear ball caps and march shirtless through the streets chanting "Uff da, Uff da," in what has become a national celebration of the baseball cap. This story, too, is patently false. The actual phrase they chant is "Uff da-Yay, Uff da-Yay."

Cap Weinberger. There are two versions of this myth—one that Weinberger was nicknamed "Cap" because he frequently wore a ball cap as a youngster; second, that the ball cap was invented by Weinberger. Neither story is true. In fact, there's no indication that he ever wore a ball cap. It is true, however, that as Richard Nixon's budget director, Weinberger earned the nickname "Cap the Knife" for his budget-cutting prowess. As President Reagan's Secretary of Defense, Weinberger presided over a record two-trillion-dollar military budget, though, and some changed the nickname to "Cap the Shovel" or "Cap the Ladle."

It is sometimes reported that the term "per capita" derives from "per cap owner"—as in income per cap owner—and that it originated with the Alabama legislature, which apparently does not differentiate between "cap owner" and "resident." A more likely explanation is the Latin definition of "per capita," which is "for each head."

"Capsize" is what happens when a boat overturns. The origins of this word are often traced to the fitted ball cap, which, when turned over, reveals the cap's size. The other use of "cap size" (as in "Hey, what's your cap size?") also derives from the ball cap. "Capsize," by the way, means literally "to sink by the head."

The term "cap in hand" was invented by Al Gore. Variations of this story attribute the phrase to Michael Jackson, Ronald Reagan, Babe Ruth, and Popeye. In fact, its earliest known use dates to 1565, when it reportedly referred to a show of respect toward a judge. Its meaning has changed over the years, so that today it means to humbly ask for a favor. It is believed that Popeye invented this current usage.

"Handicap." It is often thought that this term comes from the phrase "cap in hand," and that it alludes to begging or beggars. Actually, the phrase comes from "hand in cap" (or "hand in hat"), which has a very different origin than "cap in hand." Hand in Cap was the name of a lottery game played in Britain in the 1600s, and the term eventually came to mean an adjustment in sports contests to make a match more equitable. In horse racing, for instance, the saddles of the fastest horses were weighted so that the race would be more competitive. It was only in the early 1900s that the definition came to mean physical limitations. The other use of this term—meaning a cap that is "handy"—is spelled differently.

To "set one's cap for" someone else means to pursue that person romantically. This is true. But the phrase did not originate with Betty and Veronica, as we often hear. It comes from the French navigational expression *mettre le cap sur*, meaning "to set a course for."

TRUE OR FALSE: THE INTERNATIONAL TEST

Now it's your turn. Here are twelve brief international "cap tales." Six are true, six are false. See if you can tell which is which.

1. In 2007, Winston Churchill's granddaughter, Celia Sandys, called U.S. Republican presidential candidate Rudolph Giuliani "Churchill in a baseball cap," a reference to Giuliani's leadership after the September 11 attacks.

2. In Spain—where the baseball cap is known as *gorra de béisbol*—King Juan Carlos once wore a ball cap that glowed in the dark. The cap was a prototype developed by a Spanish apparel firm owned by a member of the royal family.

3. During his summer vacation retreats to the mountains of northern Italy, Pope Benedict XVI sometimes wears a white baseball cap.

4. German Chancellor Angela Merkel and President George W. Bush once wagered a dozen baseball caps on the outcome of the World Cup soccer tournament.

5. The famous Shakespeare line "A hat, a hat, my kingdom for a hat" is from *Richard III*.

6. In Salzburg, Austria, Wolfgang Amadeus Mozart baseball caps were sold in dozens of shops and stalls in January 2006 to mark the composer's two-hundred-and-fiftieth birthday.

7. Zimbabwe's controversial President Robert Mugabe often wears baseball caps bearing his own image.

8. "A horse is a horse, of course, of course" was a greeting recited by cap-makers in *Othello*.

9. At the Beijing Olympics in 2008, Russian pole vaulter Yelena Isinbayeva stayed focused by remaining in her room at the Olympic Village before competition. The only times she went out, she wore a baseball cap pulled over her face and dark glasses.

10. The polar ice cap was so named because of its physical resemblance to a baseball cap.

11. In May 1998, then-Indian Prime Minister Atal Bihari Vajpayee toured a nuclear test site seventy miles from the Pakistan border wearing a cap emblazoned with the word "shakti," a Hindu word for power.

12. A 2006 meeting of the G8 in Toyako, Japan, included a discussion of "Baseball Caps and the World's Labor Market."

Answers: 1 T; 2 F; 3 T; 4 F; 5 F; 6 T; 7 T; 8 F; 9 T; 10 F; 11 T; 12 F

10

BALL CAP TRIVIA

Almost everything you wanted to know about the baseball cap
(and some things you probably didn't); the official Ball Cap
Trivia Quiz; plus, an exclusive interview with
the most famous and popular ball cap in history.

WHAT did Babe Ruth sometimes place between his head and his baseball cap? How many caps does a professional baseball player go through in a season? What world leader and former U.S. president sat together at a baseball game in 2002, both wearing ball caps? What is the purpose of the button on the top of the baseball cap?

We journey now into the arcane world of baseball cap trivia ...

WHAT LIES BENEATH

If you answered cabbage leaf to the first question on the previous page, you are correct. Babe Ruth would sometimes wear a leaf of fresh lettuce or cabbage beneath his ball cap, changing the leaf every couple of innings. Why did he do this? Because it kept his head cool. Although this story has a whiff of popular mythology, it is apparently true. Baseball historian Robert Creamer references it in his book *Babe: The Life and the Legend*. In fact, many other players besides Ruth used the cabbage leaf technique at the time.

Another beneath-the-cap story takes us back to 1919—a baseball season that ended with the now infamous fixed World Series, when eight Chicago White Sox players were paid to throw the Series to the Cincinnati Reds. Casey Stengel was playing outfield for the Pittsburgh Pirates that season. He'd previously been with the Brooklyn Robins for five years, from 1912–1917. On May 25, Stengel was back in Brooklyn for a game against his old team. It was a Sunday—the first season that Sunday ball was allowed in New York state—and a near capacity crowd of twenty thousand fans was in the stands at Ebbets Field. In his first three at-bats, Stengel struck out twice and grounded out to shortstop. He was roundly booed each time he came to the plate. Before his fourth at-bat, Stengel went over to the Dodgers side to talk with his friend Leon Cadore. Cadore was a pitcher, still co-holder of the Major League Baseball record for most innings pitched in a game—twenty-six, against the Phillies, a game called a tie because of darkness.

Cadore was holding a live sparrow in his hands when Stengel reached the Brooklyn dugout. Stengel, known for his quirky sense of humor, asked if he could have it. Cadore said okay. Stengel wrapped the bird inside his baseball cap and returned to the Pirates' dugout. When he came to the plate for his fourth at-bat, Stengel waved to the crowd and was booed again. Then he tipped his cap and the sparrow flew into the air above the ball field. Stengel had literally given the crowd "the bird."

Casey Stengel took off his ball cap in 1919 and gave the crowd "the bird."

Many in attendance stopped booing when they saw what he had done. The jeers became cheers.

CAPS PER SEASON

The average Major League Baseball player goes through between four and eight caps per season, according to equipment managers Rodney McCormick of the Minnesota Twins and John Silverman of the Florida Marlins. However, the number varies quite a bit from player to player. Some change their hats every few games, while others become attached to a cap and keep it most of the season. "Some go through two, some go through a lot more," said McCormick. "Four to eight is the average."

CAP SIZE

The average hat size in Major League Baseball is $7^3/_8$. The smallest head currently in the league belongs to Washington Nationals shortstop Alex Cintron. Cintron wears a size 6. Several players wear size 8 ½—the largest cap.

TRANSPARENT VISOR

In 1895, professional baseball experimented with an idea that the game wasn't quite ready for (and, apparently, still isn't)—the transparent visor. The green-tinted, transparent-billed caps were designed to allow fielders a greater range of view while shielding their eyes from the sun's glare. At the time, baseball games were all played during the day (the first night game took place on May 24, 1935, in Cincinnati). One of those who wore this cap in 1895, according to the National Baseball Hall of Fame, was future Hall of Famer Jesse Burkett. The green visor proved a distraction, though, and the transparent bill was benched indefinitely.

In 1912, Pittsburgh Pirates manager Fred Clarke created a baseball cap with pull-down lenses attached to the bill. This was before sunglasses. Pull-down lenses were used by a number of players in the 1910s and 1920s. In 1929, mass produced sunglasses were introduced to America by Sam Foster, sold as Foster Grant.

Before the invention of sunglasses, Fred Clarke created a baseball cap with dark lenses that could be pulled down from the visor.

MESSAGES TO THEMSELVES

Speaking of bills: The under-bill of the baseball cap is the only part of the MLB baseball uniform that players are allowed to write on, and over the years many of them—particularly pitchers—have done so, penning inspirational or motivational notes to themselves, which the public never sees. These under-bill messages have included everything from "Focus" to "Have Fun" to religious symbols to the names of players' spouses, girlfriends, and children.

But under-bill message-writing became difficult in 2007, when the under-bills changed from light gray to black.

When the standard 59Fifty cap was introduced in 1954, the under-bills were green, which was considered the best color to mute the glare of the sun. This became the norm in MLB until the mid-1970s, when the Cincinnati Reds changed their under-bills from green to gray, in response to a government report advocating the use of gray tones on Navy battleships, on the grounds that it was the easiest color on the crew members' eyes. Reds star Johnny Bench wrote in his *The Complete Idiot's Guide to Baseball*, "The Reds changed the color underneath the bill of the cap from green to gray. Greens and dark colors supposedly made you angry and tense; the gray supposedly made you calmer and more focused."

Other teams followed suit and eventually all of the teams in Major League Baseball wore gray under-bills. In 1998, the California Angels broke with this tradition, changing their under-bills to black. All teams went to the black under-bill in 2007 as part of the cap redesign.

EGGS OVER EASY

The Seattle Pilots were not only one of baseball's most unique teams, they also wore one of the game's most unusual caps, as we noted earlier—featuring what were supposed to be a pair of garland leafs on the brim, but which become known as the "scrambled eggs" logo.

It was a suitable symbol for a team that lasted only one season, finished last place in its division with a 64–99 record, and played in a stadium where the water pressure was so low that the toilets wouldn't flush when attendance reached ten thousand. It was also the only team in Major League Baseball history to go bankrupt.

The Pilots entered MLB as one of two American League expansion team start-ups in 1969, the other being the Kansas City Royals (the National League expansion teams were the San Diego Padres and the Montreal Expos). Their name was intended to reflect the city's maritime heritage (although, in truth, the name Pilots barely beat out its runner-up, the Green Sox). The uniforms, too, conveyed a vague nautical theme. The caps were blue with a gold "S" on the front, a gold horizontal line underneath, and the odd insignias on the brims. The jerseys were even more bizarre—what looked like a red ship's wheel with two gold wings sticking out on either side, along with gold-trim bands on the sleeves. They resembled something that might have been created for an avant-garde community theater production of *The Ghost and Mrs. Muir*.

The Pilots were the first major league baseball team in the Pacific Northwest, though, and many people in Seattle had high hopes for their new franchise. Longtime TV and radio sportscaster Rod Belcher wrote a forward-looking fight song for the Pilots, recording it with a group he called Doris Doubleday and His Command Pilots (released on Pilotune Records). It featured these lyrics:

> *Go, Go You Pilots!*
> *You proud Seattle team,*
> *Go, Go You Pilots,*
> *Go out and build a dream*
>
> *You brought the Majors*
> *To the Evergreen Northwest*
> *Now Go, Go You Pilots*
> *You're going to be the best.*

There were indications early on, though, that the Pilots might encounter some rough seas. At the first home game, on April 11, only about eighteen thousand seats of a planned twenty-five thousand in the converted minor league stadium were ready. Some patrons had to wait three innings to be seated. Seats were added during the season but many were obstructed vision. The team was under-financed and often at odds with city officials. Its ticket and concession prices were the highest in Major League Baseball. In March 1970, just days before the start of the 1970 season, the Pilots were sold to Milwaukee and became the Brewers. There wasn't time to order new uniforms, so the Brewers made do with the old Pilots uniforms. The "S" initials were ripped from the caps and replaced with "M"s.

One of the few legacies of the Pilots' lone season was the controversial book *Ball Four*, by relief pitcher Jim Bouton. An unflattering insider's look at the sport of baseball, *Ball Four* portrayed pro-ball players as boozers, womanizers, and drug users. Bowie Kuhn, then the MLB's commissioner, called the book "detrimental to baseball," and asked Bouton to sign a statement apologizing and saying that the book was fiction. Bouton declined.

Seattle Pilots uniforms and memorabilia are now prized by collectors, with caps selling for several hundred dollars at auctions.

EXCLUSIVE: INTERVIEW WITH AN ICON

The Yankees cap is, of course, the most popular baseball cap ever worn, in part because of the mystique associated with the Yankees. First appearing on the ball field in 1909, the navy colored cap, with its famous interlocking "NY" logo, has become an American icon. But not much is really known about this legendary cap. In a rare interview, the traditionally press-shy New York Yankees Cap (NYYC) opened up with us to discuss its illustrious history.

BCN: You look different off the field.
NYYC: I hear that.

BCN: What's it like to reach a hundred?
NYYC: (Shrugs)

BCN: Supposedly, you outsell all other professional baseball caps by a significant margin.

NYYC: More than three to one, I'm told.

BCN: Why? Why have you become such an institution?

NYYC: Why? I mean, it's something you can't put into words. It's like me asking you why the sky is blue. Why the grass is green. It just is.

BCN: Okay. What can you put into words?

NYYC: What have you got?

BCN: Well, let's start with the first season you were on the field. Do you have any recollections of 1909, when the Yankees cap, as we know it today, debuted?

NYYC: Yeah, I do. But first of all, we weren't the Yankees then, okay? We were called the Highlanders up until 1913. Franchise started as the Baltimore Orioles in 1901, then we moved to New York in 1903 and became the Highlanders. And here's another thing: That interlocking logo? It was actually created in 1877 by Louis Tiffany. The glass guy? Not a lot of people know this, but it was the Tiffany company that created that logo. It was done for a medal of honor given by the New York City Police Department to the first police officer shot in the line of duty. True story. Guy named John McDowell.

BCN: Where did the name Highlanders come from, by the way?

NYYC: You're killing me with your questions. Where did the name Highlanders come from? Well, at the time, we played at one of Manhattan's highest points, in what was called Hilltop Stadium. Long gone. But even when we were the Highlanders, people used to call us the Yankees. So in 1913, they decided they better make it official.

BCN: How did the Yankees do in their first season?
NYYC: Not so good. 57–94. Seventh place in the American League.

BCN: It wasn't long before you turned things around, though.
NYYC: Wasn't long.

BCN: Some pretty amazing things have been accomplished by men wearing the Yankees cap. Do you remember most of them?
NYYC: Sure. Try me.

BCN: All right. Let's see. Who was the first New York Yankee to pitch a no-hitter?
NYYC: That would be George Mogridge. April 24, 1917. First no-hitter in Fenway Park.

BCN: Very good. Do you remember the first game ever played at Yankee Stadium?
NYYC: Of course. April 18, 1923. Yankees beat the Red Sox, 4–1. Bob Shawkey threw the first pitch. It was a ball.

BCN: We would hope so.
NYYC: An interesting thing about that day: Babe Ruth also hit the first home run in Yankee Stadium. Same day. First game ever played at Yankee Stadium.

BCN: Babe Ruth more or less ushered in the Yankee dynasty, didn't he?
NYYC: You could say that if you want. Ruth joined the team in 1920. In 1921, we went to the Series for the first time, played against the Giants. The Giants were our landlords, incidentally. They told us to move out of the Polo Grounds. You know what we did? We built Yankee Stadium across the river (chuckling).

BCN: You actually played the Giants in three consecutive World Series, didn't you, losing the first two?

NYYC: Don't rub it in, pal. We won the third one in 1923. And you know what? That was a turning point—not just for the Yankees but for the sport of baseball. And I'll tell you why. Before that, the Giants were kind of the city's iconic team. In 1923, we took that away from them, and we haven't given it up since.

BCN: Weren't you known in the twenties as Murderer's Row?

NYYC: Among other things, yeah (chuckling). That particular term actually goes back to 1918, before Babe joined us. The press invented that one.

BCN: But people associate it with 1927.

NYYC: Do they? Sure. That was a good year.

BCN: Some people say that was the best baseball team that ever played the game.

NYYC: Oh, yeah? Wonder what would make them say that? I mean, we only won the American League by nineteen games. Went 110 and 44. Had a combined batting average of .307. Outscored our opponents by 376 runs. Yeah, come to think of it, that was a pretty good team. But I wouldn't discount some of the other teams, from '39 or '98, say. Or '61, for that matter.

BCN: You won the Series in 1927, too.

NYYC: Swept the Series.

BCN: That was the year Babe Ruth hit sixty home runs, wasn't it?

NYYC: That's right. Record that stood for thirty-four years. In many people's minds, it still stands today. Sixty home runs. That was 14 percent of all the home runs hit in Major League Baseball that year.

BCN: How did Lou Gehrig do in 1927?
NYYC: Gehrig? He batted .373, had 218 hits.

BCN: The Yankees hold the record for the most consecutive World Series wins—five in a row, from 1949 to 1953. But that was a different incarnation of the team.
NYYC: Yeah, that was what some call the DiMaggio era. I'm glad you brought up that record, by the way. Here's an interesting piece of trivia: The only other team to win four Series in a row was the Yankees, too, from 1936 through 1939.

BCN: Wow. How many total World Series titles have the Yankees won?
NYYC: Total? Twenty-six. You want the years?

BCN: All right.
NYYC: 1923, 1927, 1928, 1932, 1936, 1937, 1938, 1939, 1941, 1943, 1947, 1949, 1950, 1951, 1952, 1953, 1956, 1958, 1961, 1962, 1977, 1978, 1996, 1998, 1999, 2000.

BCN: Some great players have worn the Yankees cap.
NYYC: Fact is, more numbers have been retired on the Yankees than on any other baseball team. Sixteen. I'll name them if you'd like.

BCN: Oh, okay.
NYYC: No. 1—Billy Martin; No. 3—Ruth; No. 4—Gehrig; No. 5—DiMaggio; No. 7—Mantle; No. 8—Yogi Berra; No. 8—Bill Dickey—No. 8 was retired to honor both Yogi and Dickey, okay?—No. 9—Roger Marris; No. 10—Phil Rizzuto; No. 15—Thurman Munson; No. 16—Whitey Ford; No. 23—Don Mattingly; No. 32—Elston Howard; No. 37—Casey Stengel; No. 44—Reggie Jackson; No. 49—Ron Guidry. Then, of course, Jackie Robinson's number, 42, was retired by every team in the league in 1997.

BCN: Okay, so when exactly did the Yankees cap transcend baseball? When did you begin to become an international phenomenon, rather than just part of a baseball uniform?

NYYC: Well. I've always been an international phenomenon, I'm just more so now (winks). Look, if I had to pick a date? I'd probably say '96. Okay? If I *had* to. Because in 1996, we won the Series for the first time since 1978. That's a lot of years. And in the interim, the baseball cap had become kind of a big deal in this country. So it only figures that there'd be a lot of interest in the Yankees cap. The orders for Yankee caps that year more than doubled the orders for Atlanta Braves caps the year before, which is the team that won the 1995 World Series, okay? That's according to Chris Koch, my man at New Era.

BCN: A lot of people wear Yankees caps these days who don't follow baseball.

NYYC: Sure, a lot of people think of me as representing New York *City*, not the New York Yankees. And that's all right.

BCN: Have there been many substantial changes to the Yankees cap— or the Yankees uniform—over the years?

NYYC: Substantial? Nah. You're dealing with history, my man. The Yankees uniform has basically been the same since 1936. That's longer than any other team's uniform.

BCN: You're found all over the world now, in virtually every country. And yet, some people say the Yankees ball cap represents what's wrong with America—the brash, unsophisticated, imperialistic American.

NYYC (scowling): Who says that?

BCN: Well, there was an interesting article to that effect in the *L.A. Times* a while ago, which called you "the cap of the bully."

NYYC: I don't read the *L.A. Times*. Aren't they the paper that broke the news about Britney Spears?

BCN: What news was that?

NYYC: (chuckling) I'm playing with you. Look, I don't want to get into psychological mumbo jumbo here. The Yankees are what they are, okay? But I'll say this: When you're successful, as the Yankees have been, there's always going to be people who want to tear you down. Okay? But you know what? I think the Yankee caps represent exactly what's *right* about America: drive, heart, courage, loyalty, scrappiness. Hitting the ball out of the park. Winning. You name it. And, on top of all that, we also happen to represent the largest city in the country and, some would say, the greatest city in the world. So, I mean, what do you want?

BALL CAP RECIPES

The baseball cap is such an ingrained part of our culture now that many people find it perfectly acceptable to eat baseball caps. Well, maybe not literally eat the caps. But dozens of culinary creations have emerged in recent years that use the design of the baseball cap. Both Land O' Lakes and Betty Crocker, for example, provide recipes for baseball cap cup cakes. Other culinary delicacies include chocolate baseball caps, baseball cap tacos, and ball cap cookies.

BALL CAP SOURCES

One of the best sources on sports uniforms, including caps, is Paul Lukas's blog (www.uniwatchblog.com), billed as "The Obsessive Study of Athletics Aesthetics."

Another valuable source of information about hats of all varieties is the newsletter *Hat Life* (www.hatlife.com), edited by Diane Feen.

CAPPING IT OFF

It's time now to take the **Ball Cap Trivia Quiz**. Please put away all your papers, sharpen your pencils, and allow yourself twenty-five minutes to answer the following thirty questions. Most of the questions cover information previously discussed in this book. Good luck.

(If you get twenty-eight or more correct, write to the author in care of the publisher and he will send you a signed copy of this book along with a Ball Cap Nation baseball cap.* The honor system applies.)

*While supplies last; limited offer; one winner per household; terms of this offer may change without notice; the author is not liable for any injuries or disabilities incurred by persons taking the "Ball Cap Trivia Quiz"; the author reserves the right to decline or destroy entries for any reason whatsoever; the "Ball Cap Trivia Quiz" is intended solely for amusement purposes; prizes have no cash value (unless you are able to sell them); contest winners may be subject to financial background checks, strip searches, and possible wire-tapping; contestants in the states of New York, California, and Rhode Island may be subject to an additional 33 percent "quiz tax"; all submissions become the property of the United States government; you may enter as often as you wish, however multiple entries are prohibited in some jurisdictions and subject to fines equal to but not exceeding $561,993; if you should experience swelling or skin rashes while taking the "Ball Cap Trivia Quiz," please contact your physician immediately; if you experience chest pains, you may have had a meatball sub or something similarly large and disgusting for lunch; if you didn't, please contact 911; "Ball Cap Trivia Quiz" is a registered trademark; if you try to use it, we will catch you and prosecute you, you little punk; this offer valid only on Tuesdays and Fridays between 12:30 and 2:45 p.m.; other fees may apply; all associated fees may be deducted arbitrarily from your social security account or your 401(k) plan; all decisions are final; the terms of this offer are non-negotiable.

1. In 1849, the first baseball team, the Knickerbockers, wore this on their heads:

A. straw hats
B. bowler caps
C. beanies
D. lettuce leafs

2. Baseball was invented by:

A. Abner Doubleday

B. Abner Graves

C. Alexander Cartwright

C. Henry Chadwick

E. no one person invented baseball

3. Who said, "On fortune's cap we are not the very button?"

A. Yogi Berra

B. Sean "Puffy" Combs

C. Casey Stengel

D. William Shakespeare

4. The cost of a baseball cap in 1888 was:

A. 12 cents to $2

B. $1.25–$3

C. $5–$6

D. $8.99 and $9.99

5. The most popular baseball cap of the 1880s was called the "Chicago Style." This style is also known as:

A. beanie

B. pillbox

C. skull cap

D. jockey cap

6. What purpose does the button at the top of the baseball cap serve?

A. propeller attachment

B. it hides the junction of the seams

C. none

D. it was designed to hold players' chewing gum

7. *Which of these actors was* not *known for wearing a baseball cap?*
A. Scotty Beckett
B. Jerry Mathers
C. Huntz Hall
D. Mickey Rooney

8. *The first professional baseball cap to have an image illustrating its team nickname on the crown was the:*
A. Detroit Tigers, 1902
B. Boston Beaneaters, 1890
C. Cincinnati Red Stockings, 1875
D. St. Louis Cardinals, 1907

9. *The crown of the modern-day baseball cap has how many panels?*
A. 4
B. 6
C. 8
D. 12

10. *What world leader and former U.S. president sat together at a baseball game in 2002, both wearing red caps with the letters C and A, respectively?*
A. Tony Blair and Bill Clinton
B. Vladimir Putin and Bill Clinton
C. Fidel Castro and Jimmy Carter
D. Silvio Berlusconi and George H.W. Bush

11. *Who among the following do not wear baseball caps:*
A. policemen in Slovenia
B. parachute riggers in the U.S. Army
C. referees in the National Football League
D. Federal Express delivery people

12. *The New Era Cap Company began manufacturing ball caps in:*
A. 1934
B. 1954
C. 1903
D. 1948

13. *Caps that advertise products on tall foam fronts are nicknamed:*
A. foamies
B. billboard caps
C. gimme caps
D. meshies

14. *Who said, "I pulled on a baseball cap, pulled 'er down … We looked like a normal couple"? And who was the other half of this "normal couple?"*
A. Prince Charles and Camilla Parker Bowles
B. Vince Gill and Amy Grant
C. Ellen DeGeneris and Tom Cruise
D. George W. Bush and Condoleeza Rice

15. *Which of the following caps did Tom Selleck not wear on* Magnum, P.I.?
A. U.S. Navy cap with the logo "VM02 Da Nang"
B. a red-and-white cap with the logo "Al's Collision and Muffler Shop"
C. a black Detroit Tigers cap with an *orange* old-English "D" on the crown
D. a black Detroit Tigers cap with a *white* old-English "D" on the crown
E. a light blue cap with the Playboy bunny logo

16. *The famous chef who tossed out his toques in favor of baseball caps was:*
A. Paul Bocuse
B. Wolfgang Puck
C. Alain Ducasse
D. Chef Boyardee

17. *The All-American Professional Girls Baseball League, which played from 1943 to 1954, wore baseball caps that differed from men's baseball caps because:*
A. they contained product advertisements
B. they had elastic bands on the back so that one size fit all
C. they were pink
D. they had two bills

18. *The John Deere trucker cap has been promoted by:*
A. Bruce Willis
B. Boxcar Willie
C. Aston Kutcher
D. Julia Roberts

19. *The American film director who helped create a market for "off-color" baseball caps was:*
A. Michael Moore
B. Steven Spielberg
C. Spike Lee
D. Ron Howard

20. *Who among the following hip-hop artists did not design a base-ball cap line?*
A. Ludacris
B. Fabolous
C. Lil Wayne
D. Fat Joe

21. *The person often credited with popularizing the backwards base-ball cap in America during the 1980s was:*
A. Madonna
B. Ken Griffey, Jr.
C. Spike Lee
D. Eminem

22. *Who wore a baseball cap during a 1983 event at the White House?*
A. Francois Mitterand
B. Margaret Thatcher
C. Mike Love
D. Frank Sinatra

23. *What political candidate was criticized for frequently wearing a baseball cap with his name on it?*
A. William Hague
B. Ross Perot
C. Vladimir Putin
D. Harry Truman

24. *Beginning in the eighth season of* M*A*S*H, *Klinger sometimes wore a baseball cap with a "T" on the crown. The "T" stood for:*
A. Detroit Tigers
B. Toledo Mud Hens
C. Tarrytown Tigers
D. North Carolina Tar Heels

25. *In the movie* The Departed, *Jack Nicholson wore the baseball cap of which team?*
A. Boston Red Sox
B. New York Yankees
C. New York Mets
D. California Angels

26. *Since 2007, professional baseball caps have been made of:*
A. wool
B. a wool-cotton blend
C. polyester
D. recycled newspaper

27. *If all Frooks are Dreebs and some Dreebs are Groobs, which of the following statements is true:*
A. All Groobs are Frooks
B. Some Frooks are Freebins
C. Most Frooks have short left legs
D. Euclidean geometry was invented by Rene Descartes
E. none of the above

28. *This big-league pitcher is known for sometimes wearing his baseball cap sideways on the field:*
A. J.J. Putz
B. Johan Santana
C. Takashi Saito
D. C.C. Sabathia

29. *Which French politician was famously photographed in a turquoise bikini and a dark blue baseball cap?*
A. Carla Bruni
B. Segolene Royal
C. Nicolas Sarkozy
D. Jacques Chirac

30. *The author's first little league cap had which letter on the front— and what did it stand for?*
A. S for Senators
B. B for Braves
C. M for Manor Boys
D. Q for the Quixotic
E. all of the above

Answers: 1 A; 2 E; 3 D; 4 A; 5 B; 6 B; 7 D; 8 A; 9 B; 10 C; 11 D; 12 A; 13 C; 14 D; 15 E; 16 B; 17 B; 18 C; 19 C; 20 C; 21 B; 22 C; 23 A; 24 B; 25 B; 26 C; 27 E; 28 D; 29 A; 30 C

AFTERWORD

Ball Cap Earth

When we put on a baseball cap, we feel just a little more comfortable with the world. We see it—and it sees us—a bit differently. It's a subtle thing. While politicians and diplomats seek to solve our global differences, cap-wearers point out our commonalities. We *are* a Ball Cap Nation, but we're also part of "Ball Cap Earth." The proliferation of the ball cap is not quite the same as world peace; but it's a good, hopeful sign, when people of such diverse cultures and beliefs can embrace the same thing. The ball cap has become a symbol of our better natures, a flag for a new worldwide, borderless community.

And besides all that, the cap is just plain cool.

Photo Credits

The photos on the following pages appear courtesy of the author: 15, 37, 77, 80, 89, 151

The photos on the following pages appear courtesy of the Library of Congress: 24, 141, 171, 199

The photos on the following pages appear courtesy of the Baseball Hall of Fame Library, Cooperstown, N.Y.: v, 31, 33, 92, 201

The photos on the following pages appear courtesy of iStockphoto: 49, 56, 175, 178

Dust jacket
Front cover—Ball cap, Donna Poehner, Zia Portrait Design; Bottom: First and third photos, Dreamstime; second and fourth photos, iStockphoto; fifth photo, Donna Poehner, Zia Portrait Design

Inside front flap—Photo courtesy of the Library of Congress

Back cover—Top: Photo courtesy of the Baseball Hall of Fame Library, Cooperstown, N.Y. Bottom: Photo courtesy of Jon Warren/World Vision

Inside back flap—Photo of author courtesy of Janet Johnson

Color Insert
Opening page—©James Lehmann, used with permission; second page—*Chicago Tribune* photo by Nuccio DiNuzzo. All rights reserved. Used with permission; third page—Tim Sloan/AFP/Getty Images; fourth page—clockwise: Janet Kubat, *Agri News*, Donna Poehner, iStockphoto; fifth page—Touchstone Pictures/Photofest; sixth page—CBS/Photofest; seventh page—Jon Warren/World Vision; last page—NBC, Universal Photo Bank

Other Photo Credits
p. x, Photodisc; p. 53, MGM/Photofest; pp. 69, 75, courtesy of New Era; p. 86, courtesy of Bruce Evans; pp. 108, 116, courtesy of Hat World; p. 145, AP Images/John Dunn; p. 154, Smithsonian Institution Collections, National Museum of American History, Behring Center; p.157, Mark Schilling and the Corn Palace Staff; p. 159, 2002, © M. Scott Moon; p. 172, Jack Rowell; p. 185, Jon Warren/World Vision; p.189, photo by Dion Nissenbaum, used with permission; p. 222, Janet Johnson

---

THE
BALL CAP NATION
IS ON THE WEB

Let's keep talking about ball caps!

Join the discussion at **theballcapnation.com**.

Tell us about your own caps, see cap photos, meet other

cap fanatics, and enjoy much more information about

America's national cap.

ABOUT THE AUTHOR

JAMES LILLIEFORS is an award-winning journalist and novelist whose work has appeared in the *Miami Herald*, the *Washington Post*, the *Boston Globe*, the *Baltimore Sun*, and various other publications. His books include *America's Boardwalks*, *Highway 50*, and *Bananaville*. Lilliefors grew up in the Washington, D.C., area and currently lives in Naples, Florida. He owns a large but not particularly distinguished collection of baseball caps.

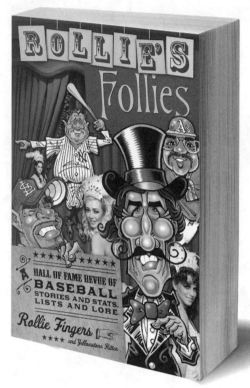